W9-BPT-007

The Story of New England is a lively account of the region and its people, from Miles Standish to John F. Kennedy. Here in words and pictures are the Pilgrims, Puritans, Minutemen, Yankee seamen, Irish and other New Englanders who have contributed to the growth of their fascinating region.

Endpaper: MARTHA'S VINEYARD

Facing Page: HARTFORD

The Story of New England

The Story of
New England

· BY MONROE STEARNS ·

illustrated with prints and paintings by
PAUL REVERE, JOHN SINGLETON COPLEY,
GILBERT STUART, WINSLOW HOMER,
and many other NEW ENGLAND *artists,*
as well as maps and photographs

RANDOM HOUSE · NEW YORK

MAP: Francis & Shaw, Inc., page 2.

PICTURES COURTESY OF: John Alden Kindred, 29; Lyman Allyn Museum, 109; American Antiquarian Society, 54, 77, 84; American Museum of Natural History, 23; Amherst College Library, 144; Bostonian Society, 49, 78, 111 left, 113, 166; Bowdoin College Museum of Art, 71; Brown Brothers, 120, 131, 132, 133, 146 bottom, 150, 151, 154, 155, 156, 158; John Carter Brown Library, 44; Cabot, Cabot and Forbes, 167; Carl Candels and Associates, back endpaper; Chase Manhattan Money Museum, 43, 64, 89 bottom; Connecticut Development Commission, 50, 170; Connecticut Historical Society, 100; Culver Pictures, 139, 143 bottom, 146 top, 153 top; Dartmouth College News Service, 70, 72 top; Dover Publications, Pictorial Archives Series, 91; Essex Institute, 35, 99 both, 117; Frick Art Reference Library, 69 bottom; Mrs. Robert H. Goddard, 157; Goodspeed's Book Shop, 69 top; Harvard University, 33, 153 bottom; Index of American Design, National Gallery of Art, v, 98 bottom; Lexington Historical Society, 83; Library of Congress, 63, 94, 96, 115 top, 123, 128, 130, 138 top, 148 bottom, 149; Magnum: (Dennis Stock) 163, (Burt Glinn) 165; Marine Historical Association, Mystic, Conn., 111 right; Massachusetts Historical Society, 19, 59 top, 61, 90; Metropolitan Museum of Art: (gift of Mrs. T. Insley Blair, 1945) 62, (bequest of A. T. Clearwater) 104 both, (gift of William H. Huntington, 1883) 92 top, (gift of Katharine Keyes, 1938, in memory of her father, Homer Eaton Keyes) 172, (bequest of Charles Allen Munn) 60, 81, 85, 88, 101, (gift of Mrs. Russell Sage) 80, (gift of I. N. Phelps Stokes, Edward S. Hawes, Alice Mary Hawes, Marion Augusta Hawes, 1937) 108 both, 114, 116 bottom, 119 bottom, (bequest of Moses Tanenbaum) 122; Montpelier, Thomaston, Maine, 93; Museum of Art, Rhode Island School of Design, 38; Museum of the American Indian, Heye Foundation, 4 both, 5, 6, 11; Museum of Fine Arts, Boston: 56, 59 bottom, 73, (bequest of Charles Francis Adams) 92 bottom, (gift of daughters of Edward D. Boit in memory of their father) 145, (on deposit courtesy of city of Boston) 76 both, 89 top, (gift of William Francis Channing) 112 bottom, (on deposit courtesy of First Church of Boston) 37, (Karolik Collection) 148 top, (gift of Mrs. Horatio Lamb in memory of Mr. and Mrs. Winthrop Sargent) 103, (gift of the Revere family) 75; National Portrait Gallery, London, 12; National Portrait Gallery, Smithsonian Institution, 115 bottom; New-York Historical Society, 66 top, 102, 107, 125, 129 top; New York Public Library, 7 both, 8 both, 10, 14, 16, 31, 40, 41, 46, 51, 55, 105, 116 top, 118, 119 top, 121, 126, 129 bottom, 136, 137, 143 top; North Carolina Museum of Art, 65; Office of the Commonwealth of Massachusetts, 34, 52; Old Sturbridge Village, 95 both, 173; Walter Osborne, 135; Peabody Museum of Salem, 98 top; Photo Researchers Inc.: (Slim Aarons) 152, (J. W. Cella) i, (George Daniell) 3, (Dick Hanley) 82, (Tom Hollyman) cover, ii, vii, 141, (George Leavens) 171, (John Lewis Stage) front endpaper; Pilgrim Society, 20, 24, 32; Plimoth Plantation, 13, 25; Preservation Society of Newport County, 74, 147; Revere Copper & Brass Inc., 97 top; Rhode Island Historical Society, 97 bottom; Smithsonian Institution, 138 bottom; Society for the Preservation of New England Antiquities, 57, 124; Ezra Stoller Associates, 169; Vermont Historical Society, 86; Wadsworth Atheneum, 106 bottom; Whaling Museum, New Bedford, 110 both, 112 top; Wide World Photos, 161; Winchester Gun Museum, New Haven, 21, 27 both; Henry Francis duPont Winterthur Museum, 42; Worcester Art Museum, 53; Yale University Art Gallery, 47, 66 bottom, 68, 87, 106 top; Yale University Library, 72 bottom.

For helpful suggestions in the preparation of this book, grateful acknowledgment is made to Mrs. Emily Holmes, Hampton, Connecticut; Mrs. P. Houlihan, Rare Book Room, New York Public Library; Daniel Leab, History Department, Columbia University; and Mrs. Davis Maraspin, Bostonian Society, Old State House, Boston. Holt, Rinehart and Winston, Inc., has kindly granted permission to reprint lines from "For John F. Kennedy His Inauguration" from *In the Clearing* by Robert Frost (copyright 1942, © 1961, 1962 by Robert Frost).

© *Copyright, 1967, by Monroe Stearns*
All rights reserved under International and Pan-American Copyright Conventions.
Published in New York by Random House, Inc., and
simultaneously in Toronto, Canada, by Random House of Canada Limited.

Library of Congress Catalog Card Number: 67-20387

Manufactured in the United States of America

Designed by Janet Townsend

· CONTENTS ·

FOR
John and Bobbie Cutler
AND
McVoy and Anna McIntyre

The Story of New England

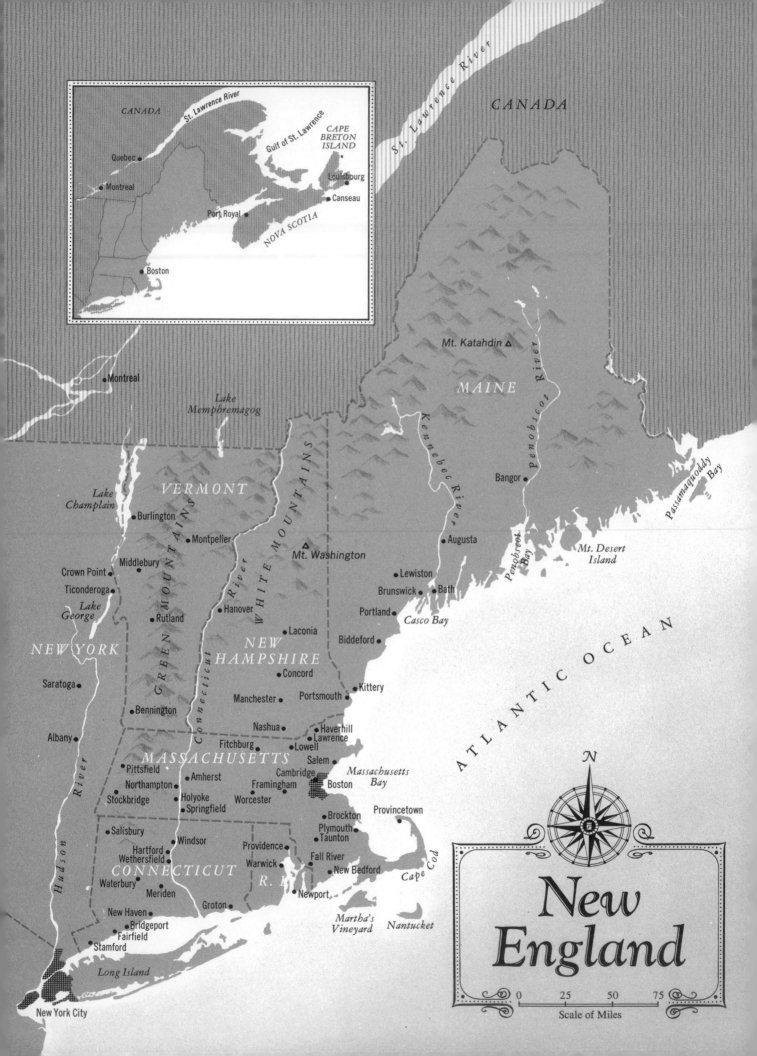

Inset map:

CANADA

St. Lawrence River

Gulf of St. Lawrence

CAPE BRETON ISLAND

Quebec

Montreal

Louisbourg

Canseau

Port Royal

NOVA SCOTIA

Boston

Main map:

CANADA

St. Lawrence River

MAINE

Mt. Katahdin △

Penobscot River

Montreal

Lake Memphremagog

Kennebec River

Bangor

Passamaquoddy Bay

VERMONT

WHITE MOUNTAINS

Lake Champlain

Burlington

Montpelier

Mt. Washington △

Augusta

Penobscot Bay

Mt. Desert Island

Crown Point

Middlebury

GREEN MOUNTAINS

Connecticut River

Lewiston

Ticonderoga

Lake George

Rutland

Hanover

Brunswick

Bath

NEW YORK

NEW HAMPSHIRE

Laconia

Portland

Casco Bay

Saratoga

Biddeford

ATLANTIC OCEAN

Concord

Manchester

Portsmouth

Kittery

Albany

Bennington

Nashua

Haverhill

Fitchburg

Lawrence

Lowell

Hudson River

MASSACHUSETTS

Salem

Pittsfield

Amherst

Cambridge

Northampton

Framingham

Boston

Massachusetts Bay

N

Stockbridge

Holyoke

Worcester

Springfield

Brockton

Provincetown

Salisbury

Plymouth

Windsor

Taunton

Hartford

Providence

Fall River

Cape Cod

Wethersfield

Warwick

New Bedford

CONNECTICUT

R. I.

Waterbury

Meriden

Newport

New Haven

Groton

Bridgeport

Martha's Vineyard

Nantucket

Fairfield

Stamford

Long Island

New York City

New England

0   25   50   75

Scale of Miles

1·THE ROADBED

In a clean Vermont village—white clapboards, red bricks, green fountains of elms—the chimes in the meetinghouse steeple break deep summer's silence with an old hymn tune.

At the head of Boston harbor skyscrapers of stone and steel catch the sun in a million windows and flash it down on thousands of cars that roar through the veins of the million-voiced city.

New Hampshire's narrow roads twine through notches of granite-faced mountains past fields where flaming Indian paintbrush half hides a plot of forgotten gravestones, amble through elm-tunneled streets flanked by cupolaed schools and colleges, flow into bustling mill towns and racetracks.

The rocky coast of Maine

3

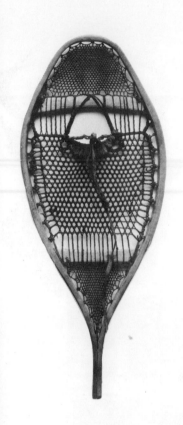

Algonquin snowshoe

Coiled basket of the Narragansett Indians of Rhode Island

Marble palaces stare haughtily from the rocks at the waves that roll into Newport from Spain, while behind, guitars twang and drums pound and clarinets shrill for the rock-and-rollers.

The pines and balsams of Maine peer into a mirror-smooth lake where a moose laps the pure icy water and a loon on an island looses his crazy laughter. The same primeval forest flanks meager fields where poverty-pinched farmers grub the thin sandy soil for bare livings. Farther off, fishing smacks hug tarry wharves piled with lobster pots and hung with nets.

The land itself is the body of New England, so scrawny that the bones of the planet stick through. The New England spirit which dwells in it is strong as steel. The two elements conflict, as body and spirit are said to do in a human being. They have reacted on each other as dramatically as an acid reacts on a base. The result is the salty New England Way.

The region man's politics has defined as New England once lay under the sea. Many times, heat and pressure at the core of the earth thrust up the land into mountains that the sun and wind, the rain and the ice wore away. The air was hot. Even the cold peak of Maine supported plants and animals of a kind now found only in the tropics.

Then ice sheets extinguished and buried that first life, tore down or flattened the mountains, swept the debris before them eastward and southward, dropped it at the edge of the sea. Under this tremendous, unevenly distributed weight of soil and rock, the land itself sank. The sea flowed in where it could, carving out hundreds of inlets, coves, harbors, and bays. They give New England a lacelike border. Some deposits rose high, making the hundreds of islands that speckle the offshore waves.

In the Gulf of Maine the sweepings of the glaciers extended the land into a shelf under the water. Plants could grow there that fish could feed on, for the water was shallow and the sun could pierce it. Fish thrived and multiplied on these "banks," the rich bequest of the glaciers.

When the ice sheets melted, as the climate grew warm again, they left New England strewn with boulders and stones. Its soil was thin, and beneath it were none of earth's riches—only a little iron, less copper, mere traces of other valuable minerals, no oil, no coal. The sea held New England's natural wealth and its road to more.

Human beings came later, not much over three thousand years ago. They came first from Asia, then moved eastward into New England. The first ones there hunted and fished; they could work with wood; and they had some kind of religion. That is all that we know of these people. Their story is told by the slate spear points, plummets, hatchet and adze blades, and the stone figures they left. They have been called the Red Paint People because they filled graves with red ocher (powdered iron ore).

After them came Indians of the Algonquin language group, a more advanced people. They, too, were in the Stone Age culture, but they also made vessels of pottery and wood, birch-bark boxes, baskets of willow and reed, fiber mats and blankets, ropes and nets. They hunted with bows and arrows, negotiated the water in birch-bark canoes, protected their feet with moccasins and rawhide boots —hand crafts that have yet to be bettered. They knew how to trap and snare game, how to fish through the ice, how to get over the snow with snowshoes and toboggans.

Deer mask used by the Penobscot Indians of Maine

They lived in oblong or beehive-shaped shelters sometimes large enough for twenty persons. They built these of bent saplings and covered them with mats made of rushes. They burned down the forest trees, and around the stumps planted corn, beans, tobacco, pumpkins, and squash.

These agricultural people knew enough to rotate crops and let their clearings sometimes lie fallow. What food they raised they varied with such natural delicacies as partridge, venison, turkey, fish, oysters, clams, blueberries and strawberries. Recipes for succotash, baked beans, steamed clams, elderberry wine, Indian pudding—all traditional New England dishes—came originally from these tribes.

They decorated their pottery and trimmed their clothing with beadwork and porcupine-quill designs, and they wore necklaces and bracelets—part of the artistic inheritance of New England. Their religion was fear of the forces of nature, whose aid they tried

5

to invoke and whose hostility they tried to appease. Their political system divided them into tribes according to location—generally where there was good farming or hunting and fishing. The principal tribes of New England were the Abenakis of Maine, New Hampshire, and Vermont; the Wampanoags and Massachusetts of Massachusetts and Rhode Island; the Pequots of Connecticut. A chief or sachem ruled each tribe, helped by *pineses* (warriors and councilors). They had a certain sense of honor and obligation, but none of private ownership.

Since the Algonquins left no written records of their existence before Europeans described them, they belong to the prehistory of New England.

New England's history begins when Leif Ericsson and his crew of thirty-five Vikings sailed down the coast to an island they called Vinland (possibly Martha's Vineyard or Nantucket). The year is thought to be A.D. 1000.

Wampanoag necklace of poke root

About ten years later, other Vikings kept a settlement there for three or four years, and shipped furs back to Greenland and Norway. Then trouble with the Indians, whom the Vikings called "skraellings," and among themselves, made them give up the colony. Nothing authentic has yet been found of their stay or of other alleged visits to the mainland, but a recently discovered map proves that the Viking legends which tell of the experience are not pure invention.

For nearly five hundred years after Leif Ericsson's Vikings left Vinland, there is no reliable record of any visitor to New England.

Then in 1497 John Cabot, an Italian explorer commissioned by King Henry VII of England, sailed along the coast from Cape Breton Island as far south as Cape Hatteras, and took possession of the land in the name of England. The kings of England therefore claimed that they owned the land.

Cabot brought back to Europe news of the basketfuls of fish he had caught off the shores of Nova Scotia and Maine. Fishermen from almost all the nations of Europe were moving westward from their old grounds off Iceland to fill their boats with the limitless treasures of these waters. For in Catholic Europe there was a constant demand for fish that could be dried or salted for the

Fig. 2.

hundred-odd days in every year when the faithful ate no meat.

Later fishermen came in January or February and located near a harbor where they could land their catch to clean, dry, and salt it, and also extract oil from fish livers. They built cabins, wharves, and racks. They traded with one another and with the natives, whom they called Indians because Columbus so named them when he thought he had reached India. The fishermen brought hogs to eat the fish refuse, and goats, cows, and sheep with which to feed themselves. Hence the names of several Maine islands: Hog, Ram, Cow.

In August the fishermen went home. Hence these first settlements in New England—Monhegan, the Damariscove Islands, Pemaquid, the islands of Casco Bay, Arrowsic, the Isles of Shoals, and land at the mouth of the Kennebec River—can be hardly be called permanent. It is impossible to date them accurately.

In the wake of the fishing boats came the ships of the explorers —English, Dutch, French, Portuguese. At first their captains searched for a new sea route to the wealth of the Indies, for the Moslems had closed the land routes to the Christians of Europe.

Catching, drying, and salting fish on the American coast

7

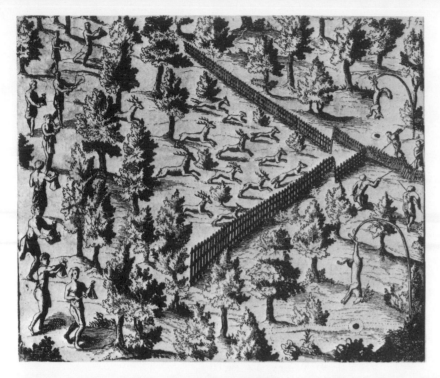

Champlain explored widely
throughout northeastern
America. His book (1619)
shows the ingenious Indian
methods for catching deer,
rabbits, and other game
(left). The picture below
shows Champlain's men at-
tacking an Indian village with
firearms. Their Indians allies
are using a torch as well as
bows and arrows.

Then, as more and more discoverers touched on the shores and brought back reports and samples of the fortunes to be had there from furs and sassafras (then thought a sure cure for many diseases) as well as fish and lumber, the merchants of Europe learned that a good substitute for the riches of the East lay in these new lands of the West.

Throughout the century after Cabot's discoveries, the nations of Europe were so occupied with internal political problems and wars with one another that they made no real attempt to found permanent settlements in America to develop its resources.

The last years of the struggle (1588-1609) saw France, England, and Holland more or less victorious over Spain. Then they began to fight among themselves. During this struggle for power in Europe a new theory of economics developed. It is called mercantilism. The gist of this theory is the enrichment of a nation and the impoverishment of its competitors. The nations tried to sell more than they bought in order to keep their money at home. They had found that the less they had to buy abroad, the safer they were in time of war.

Colonies could supply the mother country with materials which otherwise had to be bought elsewhere. Colonies would also be an outlet for the increasing populations of these countries. The establishment of colonies in North America, therefore, became an important factor in preserving the mother country's financial independence.

French explorer Samuel de Champlain established trading stations in Maine at the mouth of the St. Croix River and on Mt. Desert Island, as well as one in Nova Scotia. Largely because of the Indians' hostility the Maine stations failed. Champlain convinced his king, Louis XIII, that France's colonial empire should be built to the west, along the St. Lawrence River.

The French claims challenged the claims of England to the region. The disputes were finally adjusted, though not before an English war party from Virginia had wiped out the French settlement on Mt. Desert. But the French remained a threat to the English settlements in New England until late in the eighteenth century.

Penobscot Indians at the mouth of the Kennebec River, as shown in a book by a Dutch explorer (1651). European artists sometimes pictured American Indians as wearing East Indian clothing.

The Dutch set up trading posts near Albany, later purchased Manhattan Island, and claimed land eastward to the Connecticut River. The Dutch, however, lived in peace with their English neighbors, and did not press the Connecticut claims.

The development of New England, therefore, was the work of the English.

By the end of the sixteenth century, England was politically secure and had a solid economy at home, but was not yet a first-class power. She needed greater markets for her goods, chiefly wool and the industrial products her supply of coal made possible. The English merchants called for expansion in North America to provide the mother country with raw materials for these industries. The English also had a patriotic urge to block Spain's ambitions in the new world, and to extend English Protestantism to its inhabitants. There was also a need to get England's restless unemployed out of the country; they were increasing the crime rate. And there was plenty of money to be made from America's furs and fish and lumber.

The risks and the costs of establishing settlements for developing the resources of America were too high for a single merchant to take. So the merchants formed companies in which the public could buy stock. A company would then have enough capital to finance the cost of transporting settlers and providing them with the materials they needed to start a colony, and the risks would be shared. The company would have exclusive rights to the products of the colony and some authority in its management.

Such a company of merchants, like a corporation or a bank today, had to get from the government a charter stating its proposed methods of operation and its obligations. Since the king of England claimed ownership of the land, a charter was also a kind of lease.

King James I granted the first charters in 1606. One was to some merchants of London for development of the territory 100 miles inland from the Atlantic coast of America and from the 34th to the 41st parallel north latitude (roughly from Cape Hatteras to present New York City). The other was to some merchants of Plymouth for the territory between the 38th and 45th parallels (roughly from Washington, D.C., to Calais, Maine). There had to be two charters because the London merchants and the Plymouth merchants were deadly rivals.

The London Company founded the colony of Virginia in 1607. But no one knew much about how to start and run a colony. There was not enough capital. Management by the Company in England could not foresee or cope with problems 3,000 miles away. The settlers were more interested in personal profit than in being mere Company employees. Most of them were not hardy or persistent enough to deal with the wilderness anyway. All these factors made the colony of Virginia a financial failure.

Sir Ferdinando Gorges had been a soldier. He was only about forty years old in 1606. He was governor of the important fishing and trading port of Plymouth. He was rich and he had rich and powerful friends, notably Sir John Popham, lord chief justice of England. Gorges eagerly listened to captured Indians who had been brought to Plymouth, and believed their stories of the wealth of their homelands. He dreamed of making England greater and richer, and of ruling an empire in the new world for his king.

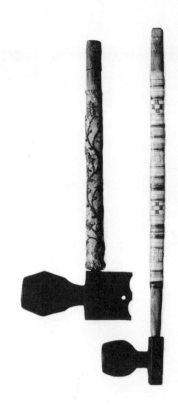

Stone pipes of the Penobscot Indians. The stems are decorated with porcupine quills.

In 1607 Gorges and Popham sent Popham's nephew George with 120 colonists to establish a colony at the mouth of the Sagadahoc (Kennebec) River, a region which they had had explored two years earlier by Captain Martin Pring. There, on August 19, this expedition established the first English government in New England. They built a fort and storehouse.

Then the winter "froze our hopes to death," as Gorges put it. All but forty-five settlers went home. George Popham died. A fire, troublesome Indians, the hasty decisions and fierce temper of their new leader wore down the rest. In the spring of 1608 they dismantled the fort they had built and sailed away.

The colony of Sagadahoc confirmed the English rights to the whole territory, for Englishmen now had actually occupied the land, however briefly. England could thus refute French claims to the region, for the French did not make a "permanent" settlement in North America until 1608.

In 1614 Captain John Smith explored the Plymouth Company's grant and reported on better places for a colony. Smith mapped the coast from Penobscot Bay to Cape Cod, named the area New

England, and christened one of its harbors Plymouth. He returned to England with a rich cargo of fish and furs, and in 1616 published a favorable report on the potential of the area for settlement —"A Description of New England."

On the strength of Smith's opinion that someone ought to start a colony there, Gorges sent Captain Richard Vines to the Maine coast. Vines found a civil war going on among the Indians, and a terrible plague also helping to wipe them out. Vines and his sixteen men spent the winter of 1616-17 at Winter Harbor (Biddeford Pool), and returned with good reports. Vines later returned to settle the area.

In 1620 Gorges reorganized the old Plymouth Company into the Council for New England. King James I granted it a charter that gave it title to all land between the 40th and 48th parallels of latitude. Gorges so dominated this Council that it was nicknamed the "gorgeous affair."

Later the Council gave Gorges and his chief associate, John Mason, rights to the land in a region known as Laconia (the present states of Maine, New Hampshire, and Vermont). Mason got the territory which now includes Vermont and New Hampshire; Mason called it New Hampshire. Gorges got an area he called Maine. Their titles to these lands were later confirmed by the English king.

King James I

After Mason's death in 1635, bitter disputes over the land titles led to New Hampshire's becoming a royal province with a governor appointed by the king of England. Gorges, and later his son Thomas, administered Maine with almost absolute power and authority until Sir Ferdinando died in 1647. Then Maine became self-governing and put itself under the jurisdiction of the Massachusetts Bay Colony.

While Gorges' Council for New England was negotiating its charter, an enterprising hardware merchant, Thomas Weston, organized his own company of merchant adventurers, chartered the *Mayflower,* and persuaded the Pilgrims to sign for transportation to New England.

2 · POOR LITTLE PLYMOUTH

Mayflower II, *a modern full-scale replica of the original* Mayflower

"Land!" came the cry from the lookout.

The sailor's call held a question. Pale morning light had just broken the darkness. The early November sky was gray and sullen. For sixty-four days the thirty-odd members of the crew and the approximately 102 passengers crowded on the 180-ton *Mayflower* had longed for a glimpse of earth. Now none could be sure that his eyes mirrored truth, not hope alone.

A moment later a shout: "Land ahoy!"

The company rushed to the rails of the vessel. The faint line grew stronger. Even those who had hesitated to trust their sight for fear of disappointment could no longer doubt that land at last was near. Their feelings burst control. Some wept. Some laughed. Some fell on their knees to praise God who had given them once again the sight of land.

For still another day the *Mayflower*'s decks pitched and rolled. She was off the dunes near Truro, where Cape Cod's fist bends inward.

William Bradford, the Pilgrims' own historian, says they had

As New England was explored and settled, details were added to John Smith's map of 1614. By 1632, when this version was published, the Charles River had been explored and charted. The map is decorated with a whale, a school of fish, huts, and a "lyon."

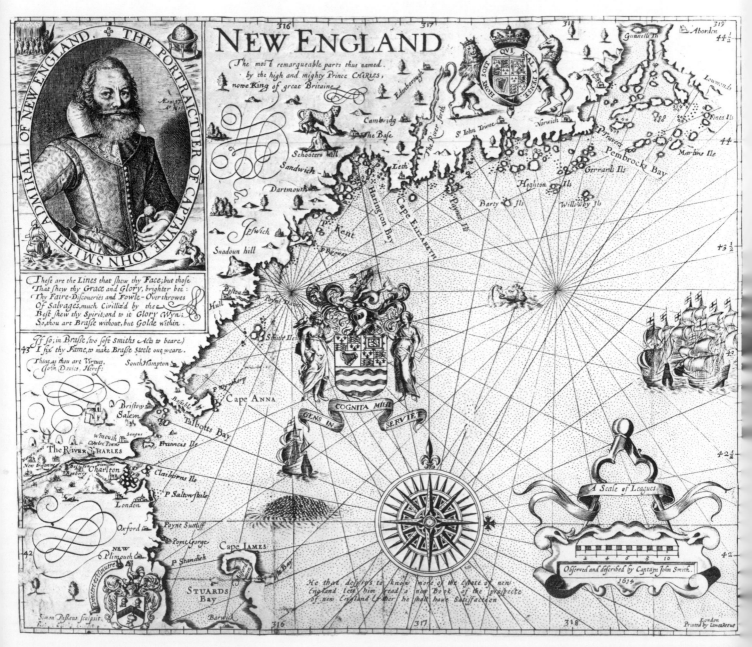

expected "to find some place about Hudson's River for their habitations."

The leaders conferred among themselves, then with the *Mayflower*'s Captain Christopher Jones. The captain turned his ship southward, then westward. About noon they reached the elbow of the Cape, off Chatham, where the water seethed and roared over shoals. The wind dropped. The waves carried them straight toward the treacherous shallows.

Perhaps leaders and captain again conferred. Probably they agreed that they might as well go back to where they had made their first landfall. After all, they knew that Captain John Smith had said someone ought to make a colony in that area.

Captain Jones put his ship about and steered her northward. He lay to for a night in the open sea. Then a fair following breeze carried the *Mayflower* round the tip of Cape Cod to drop anchor in the harbor of Provincetown, Massachusetts.

It was early on Saturday morning, November 11, 1620. The "weighty voyage" was done. Those who "knew they were pilgrims" took comfort at the sight of so good a land, wooded to the brink of the sea, and were joyful. Even so, more than one must have sighed, for they had no friends to welcome them, no inns to entertain them or refresh their weatherbeaten bodies, no towns or even houses to repair to, to seek for succor.

They would not be called "The Pilgrims" until over two hundred years later. They referred to themselves as "the Saints," meaning that they had proved to one another that they were true believers in Christ and so had been sanctified (sainted) by membership in His church, as they conceived that body to be. For they held strictly to the words of Jesus: "Where two or three are gathered together in my name, there am I in the midst of them" (Matthew 18:20).

Among the sects of seventeenth-century England, they were known as Separatists, for they had separated themselves from the established Church of England, the only legal religious body of their homeland. For setting up their own congregations, many who believed in this way of life had been clapped into jails or hanged on gallows. In the eyes of the law they were subversives, rebels,

15

traitors. They could not legally leave the country. Yet, they believed, they could not save their souls if they obeyed forms of worship or creeds imposed and enforced by other authority than their own. For freedom to believe as they chose, they stole away from their homes in and around the village of Scrooby in Nottinghamshire in the east-central part of England. They knew that only when a man can choose for himself is he truly free.

Their pilgrimage had begun twelve years before the *Mayflower* dropped anchor at Provincetown. They had gone for refuge first to Amsterdam, then to Leiden. In Holland they clung together like a primitive tribe—for in this kind of integrity they believed their preservation lay—and would not become citizens of Holland. So they made it hard for themselves to get work. Then they saw the strength of the tribe weaken, for the young kept picking up Dutch words and Dutch ways and became strangers to their elders. War between Holland and Spain threatened. The Saints chose to move on.

A romantic view of New England and its Indians, from one of John Smith's books

They were simple souls. Their various callings—tailors, weavers, cloth workers, printers, carpenters, shopkeepers—kept them poor and humble. Out of their economic and social and spiritual bondage they projected a glorious dream of freedom. To make the dream real drove them like a burning ambition. Without the dream they would have perished in the disasters that had already beset them or those which lurked ahead.

They had heard and read about free land in the new world across the sea. There they might be free to keep their agreement—their covenant—with one another to live by the word of God as they chose to interpret it.

They were also too literal to see that the reports they read were exaggerated advertisements. Even Captain John Smith's was designed to lure settlers whose labor would develop the land for the merchants who had got rights to it from the English king.

The merchants were shrewd real-estate operators. They knew how to sell the landless, the oppressed, the poverty-ridden. One of the shrewdest was Mr. Thomas Weston.

Mr. Weston went to Leiden. He persuaded the Saints that this "New England" would be a good place for them. His company would advance them the cost and the means of transportation, and supplies until they were self-sufficient.

If Mr. Weston said anything about the hazards of founding a colony in New England, the Saints paid no heed. It did not occur to them that what skills they had would be useless in a wilderness. God would provide as He had provided for His ancient chosen people who had made a covenant with Him when they too were wanderers in a wilderness. When Mr. Weston assured them that in New England the established Church had no power to harass them, they decided to go to his region, though the precise location of their settlement stayed vague.

Then they argued and argued about terms with Mr. Weston's company, particularly regarding ownership of the ground they would till. Finally they sailed without any legal charter—they were never able to get one—and with no clear financial arrangements with the merchants.

The Saints were too few to start a colony by themselves. Only forty-one finally sailed on the *Mayflower*. They were also too poor to hire a ship for their exclusive use. Mr. Weston's company of merchants knew this. They enlisted some sixty others of England's poor, and sent them along as a kind of guarantee that a revenue-producing settlement could be established. They seemed better trained for the work of founding one, more practical and less stubborn, than the Saints from Leiden.

In England these sixty men and women and children could never own their own fields. The ones they rented were being whittled away by the landowners as England changed from a farming to a sheep-raising economy. They hoped for a place where they could improve their financial and social condition rather than for one where they could improve their chances of heaven. They were of a different way of life, mostly Church of England people (Anglicans). The Saints called them Strangers.

The Pilgrims, therefore, were both Saints and Strangers.

The Strangers outnumbered the Saints, but the Saints had dealt with the merchants and thus had made the whole expedition possible. All during the long voyage the Saints kept laying down the rules for the society they were going to establish. Now that all had reached the shores of hope, the Strangers began to seethe with mutiny against rules that gave them little voice in how things would be run there.

The leaders of the Saints had to act and act fast. The crew of the *Mayflower* had no wish to tarry. Put these Psalm-singers ashore, the sailors demanded of Captain Jones, and head for home before the food is gone and the winter gales have gathered. Once ashore, both Saints and Strangers knew, they would be outside the law of the captain and the laws of England. Anyone could do as he wished. There must be some code, some covenant, a Word.

The leaders of the Saints were John Carver and William Brewster and William Bradford and Edward Winslow.

Carver was a relatively rich man and therefore the highest of the Saints in the social scale. They respected him. They had no other way of ranking a man. William Bradford said Carver was "a pious, faithful, and very beneficial instrument." With Robert Cushman, who did not cross the sea until later, Carver had handled —and somewhat bungled—the transactions with the company of merchants underwriting the whole venture.

Brewster was an educated man. He had been the loyal secretary of Sir William Davidson, one of Queen Elizabeth I's secretaries of state. Thus he had seen some of the great world before returning home from Elizabeth's splendid court to be postmaster of Scrooby —a more important job than the title implies today. He also ran a tavern there. The royal messengers of the post, whose needs he served, kept him in touch with the outer world. Brewster was converted to the Separatist way. He let the congregation meet in his tavern. For this illegal hospitality he lost his job. He was jailed and fined twenty pounds (the equivalent of about one thousand dollars today).

Released, Brewster followed the Saints to Leiden. They elected him an Elder, that is, a ruler of their congregation but not a preacher. In Holland he set up a printing press and issued tracts against the corruption of the Church of England and its priests— a business that made him hunted in England. He barely escaped the law in Plymouth, England, to sail on the *Mayflower* on September 6, 1620, when he was about fifty-three years old.

When Edward Winslow went to London as the Pilgrims' ambassador in 1651, he had his portrait painted in court clothes. This is the only surviving portrait of a Mayflower *passenger of 1620.*

Bradford was a self-educated orphan, who had endured a miserable childhood with his grandfather and later with his uncles. Doubtless this was why he saw in the congregation of the Separatists the home—and in Brewster the father—he had not known. Brewster practically adopted this youngster; they were dear friends all their life. In Leiden, where he wove cloth, Bradford lived with the Brewsters. He gave up his rights to an inheritance to cling to the cause of the Pilgrims. He was to be their governor for over thirty years and would write the pungent, pithy record of their early years in America, *Of Plymouth Plantation.*

Edward Winslow's conscience caused him to leave his upper-class family in the west of England for the word and the way of the humble Separatists. He was a printer too, and he worked with Bradford in his Leiden shop. He had "a very active genius" and he would serve the Plymouth colonists well as their ambassador, business agent, assistant governor, and governor.

*Rapier of the type carried by
Miles Standish*

These men found some secluded spot on the *Mayflower* and decided on the terms of a written document. Probably William Brewster wrote its two hundred words, which they then read to the whole company: "We whose names are underwritten . . . covenant and combine ourselves together into a civil body . . . to enact, constitute, and frame such just and equal laws . . . from time to time, as shall be thought most meet and convenient for the general good of the Colony, unto which we promise all due submission and obedience."

The Saints signed first, in order of their rank in society. Women, having no legal status whatever, were excluded. There was an anxious, silent moment as the men waited to see whether the Strangers would join them. But such was the power of the Word to bring order that it stilled the Strangers' mumbling against the rule of the Saints. One by one most of them added their names, all on the same eleventh of November.

Then they chose 45-year-old John Carver governor. He was the first freely elected official of the new world.

Under the covenant they had signed, the Mayflower Compact, a new strong tribe would march into the wilderness. It would be a free tribe. The document itself, which has long since disappeared, was signed aboard the ship before any had set foot ashore. So there would never be on that new land a trace of the old system of society which gave them no choice in the way they were ruled. Forever after, Saints and Strangers, their children and their children's children could be free to choose their governors and their laws from generation to generation.

And so at last, in orderly fashion, trusting in one another, the thankful people went ashore—the women to wash, the men to repair the *Mayflower*'s longboat and to explore New England.

For three weeks they tested the land and waters around the anchorage. Then on December 20, the Pilgrims chose to make a settlement at Plymouth, across Cape Cod Bay from Provincetown. On December 25 they began to build houses of board chinked with clay and roofed with a thatch of rushes. The day was no holiday for the Saints, who did not observe Christmas or any other festival of the established Church. It was just another Monday to them.

Many were already sick. They had been drenched with rain and sea water that coated their clothing with ice. Racking coughs slowed their work. On the tightly packed *Mayflower* infection spread, for they could not leave the ship until there were shelters on land. Governor John Carver forbade the captain to sail, and Captain Jones had pity and obeyed.

Of the Saints only William Brewster seems to have wholly escaped the sickness, and of the Strangers only Miles Standish.

Miles Standish led the Strangers in signing the Compact. He was a soldier; he knew the need of subordinating the individual to the command. But he had not risen in the army, where advancement was bought rather than earned, and so had left it for a field where his sense of his own worth would be acknowledged. He claimed to be an heir to rich estates in England from which he had been unfairly kept. These, however, seem to have existed only in his imagination. He was red-haired and florid-faced. He was also intelligent and, for his day and status, well read. He dreamed of being the Julius Caesar of his time; he left a well-thumbed copy of Caesar's *Commentaries*. Like Caesar, Standish was short, and he was bold and aggressive and supremely tactless. But without his swaggering practicality, the company might have perished.

Half of the company were dead before March was out. Those who survived the sickness—probably pneumonia and tuberculosis, aggravated by scurvy—had scarce the strength to bury the dead in unmarked graves on the hill, later called Cole's, above the shoreline of Plymouth Harbor.

It was their spirits that were strong, fortified by the love they bore one another and the faith they shared. The hale nursed the sick and did their chores "willingly and cheerfully, without grudging in the least, showing their true love unto their friends and brethren"—so William Bradford says. They had even cared for the sick boatswain of the *Mayflower* who had cursed and scoffed at them. "You, I now see," he said before he died, "show your love like Christians indeed, but we let one another die like dogs."

Mr. Weston and the company of merchants had required the Pilgrims to set up a communal society. Every man was to work for the community four days a week, and only two for himself. Each

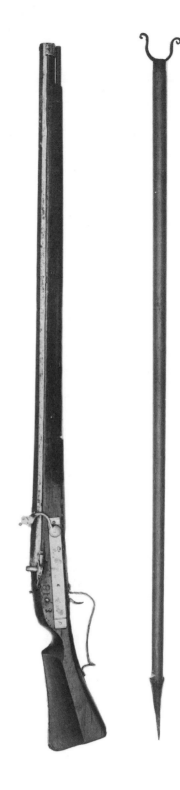

Matchlock gun of the type used by Miles Standish. The heavy gun rested on the iron support, as shown on page 8.

21

some forty miles to the southwest of Plymouth along the shores of Narrangansett Bay. Hobomuk acted as a kind of liaison man between the Wampanoags and the Pilgrims.

In April, 1621, the *Mayflower* sailed for England, taking away from the few and sickly colonists their last tie with home.

The women watched the ship drop over the horizon, and wept. They, perhaps, had a harder time of it than the men, who could work off their tensions in back-breaking labor, leaving their wives to brood on the desolateness of their new home and to long for the things they loved across the wide waters.

Longfellow's nineteenth-century poem "The Courtship of Miles Standish" is almost pure fiction. But he doubtless came near the feelings of these women when he had young Priscilla Mullins sigh that spring that she was "dreaming all night and thinking all day of the hedgerows of England. They are in blossom now, and the country is all like a garden."

The Carver chair, named for the Pilgrims' first governor, became popular throughout New England.

When Priscilla looked out her doorway in Plymouth she saw only the wilderness, heard only the cries of the hawks, the crows, and the eagles. There were no songbirds then in New England, and no flower-filled meadows.

Poor Dorothy Bradford, William's young wife, drowned from the anchored *Mayflower*. Perhaps she dropped herself over the side of the ship rather than stare longer at the wild thickets on the weather-beaten shore.

Bradford married again, and Priscilla married the "hopeful young" John Alden and bore him nine children.

A week after the *Mayflower* left, Governor Carver died of a sunstroke. The Pilgrims elected William Bradford to succeed him.

Bradford was younger, only thirty-two years old, and less set in the old ways of the Separatists—rigid, literal and hence argumentative, defensive, hesitant. His election was the second stroke of good luck. Bold and brave and energetic, practical and quick-witted, he saved the colony by his knack of adjusting constructively to situations as they arose. He believed that God's wishes for His chosen people change, and that the people must change with them.

The summer brought a good crop of corn on the twenty acres the Pilgrims had planted as Squanto taught them. But their

barley was only indifferent, and their peas a total failure.

The harvest in, Governor Bradford sent four good shots after wildfowl for a feast of rejoicing at the fruit of his people's labors. For once everyone had permission to relax. Out of gratitude they invited their good friend Massasoit to join them for the fun. He showed up with ninety of his braves. Embarrassed, the Pilgrims had to explain that they had not planned for quite so many guests. So Massasoit sent his men out for deer. They returned with five.

Miles Standish put on a military review. There were games. There was wild grape wine. The party lasted three days.

This was the first Thanksgiving. In the account of it in the chronicle of the Pilgrims' first year at Plymouth—written by Bradford and Winslow and called *Mourt's Relation* for the man who sponsored its publication in London—there is no specific mention of turkeys; but probably this traditional bird was part of the feast. No date is given for the celebration; it was probably in late September or early October. Thanksgiving did not become a national holiday until 1863, but before then it was unofficially observed in New England.

Thatching the roof of a Pilgrim house, as reconstructed at Plymouth Plantation. Each house had one main room, and the children slept in the loft.

A year after the *Mayflower* had dropped anchor off Province-town, the *Fortune* sailed into Plymouth Harbor, bringing supplies and new, young settlers, mostly Strangers. The older Strangers had been clamoring for more private property, insisting that the common lands be divided among them. Deacon Robert Cushman, who had come on the *Fortune,* preached to them on "The Dangers of Self-Love." He had to persuade the Pilgrims to sign an agreement about land titles with Mr. Weston and the company of merchants. If Cushman failed, the exasperated merchants would stop their support of the colony. Competition, selfish ambition, and pride of possession—these, Cushman thundered, were the work of the Devil.

Cushman shamed the greedy grumblers into silence—temporarily, at least. The Pilgrims were still too few and too insecure in their momentary victory over the wilderness to survive without the unity of spirit and effort that had so far preserved them. Even the discontented could see that they must stick together.

They loaded the *Fortune* with lumber and beaver skins, and sent her back to appease Mr. Weston and the company of merchants, who had been very sarcastic over the empty hold on the *Mayflower*'s return voyage. (But the French captured the *Fortune*'s cargo, and later the Pilgrims learned that they were as much in debt as ever.)

Then rumors came that in Virginia the Indians had massacred some three or four hundred settlers. The Pilgrims had found that they dared not trust even their friendly Indians. They caught Squanto in double-dealing.

Blustering Miles Standish mustered and drilled a tiny army, built a stockade, fortified the Common House where provisions were stored. The Pilgrims marched to meeting in military formation, each man with a loaded flintlock in one hand, a Geneva Bible in the other.

Standish heard that the Massachusetts tribe of Indians were threatening to destroy the settlement Weston had planted in 1622 at Wessagusset (Weymouth, some twenty miles north of Plymouth). With eight armed men and Hobomuk as interpreter, he sailed to Wessagusset, lured the Indians to a feast, killed six and

Illustrations from a manual of arms of Miles Standish's day. The military man lit his gunpowder with a slow-burning cord.

hanged one for treachery. He cut off the head of the Indian brave Wituwamat and brought it back to Plymouth, and jammed it on a spike and stuck it atop the fort. It stayed there for years as a warning.

Other troubles came with new English settlers in New England. The aristocratic lawyer Thomas Morton took over the colony which he and Captain Wollaston had set up in 1625 (near Quincy) some twenty-five miles to the north. Morton changed its name from Wollaston to Ma-re Mount (or Mountain-by-the-Sea). Then he and his young bachelor associates celebrated this re-christening with a fine feast and revels with Indian women about a Maypole.

The Pilgrims abhorred the very thought of a pagan Maypole. It was one of the English customs which had driven them from Scrooby. They promptly decided the name of Morton's settlement meant Merrymount.

Governor Bradford's common sense told him such merry doings at Merrymount might lure away the Saints' servants, who were working out the cost of their passage on the *Mayflower*—and perhaps even some of the young Saints. Worse, Morton was giving the Indians firearms and strong drink; hence, he was getting better trade in skins. Bradford told Morton to stop.

Morton only sneered at the Pilgrims' protest. Captain Standish—"Captain Shrimp," the witty Morton called him because of his short stature and florid complexion—took action.

27

With an army of nine, Standish marched to Merrymount. He would put an end to this frisking and frolicking "like so many fairies, or furies rather."

Whatever happened in the skirmish—as might be expected, Morton and Standish reported it quite differently—Standish brought Morton a prisoner to Plymouth. Standish raged that Morton should be hanged, but the more tolerant Saints merely ordered him shipped back to England. Naively they believed that no one there would ever again engage so unworthy a person to make another settlement. That was the end of Merrymount, but within a year Morton was back in New England.

The Pilgrims' trade with the Indians in beaver and otter skins began to flourish. Edward Winslow went north and set up a trading post at Cushnoc (Augusta, Maine) on the Kennebec River. The Pilgrims established another at Aptuxcet (Bourne, Massachusetts). They supported Edward Ashley's fur-trading venture at Pentagoet (Castine, Maine). Then Winslow went west and founded a post at Matianuck (Windsor, Connecticut).

Ships came regularly now from England, brought new settlers, took back skins and cedar wood. Mr. Weston kept clamoring for fish, but the Pilgrims were poor fishermen. They had come without nets and proper fishhooks. Though they had plenty now from irate Mr. Weston, they left the riches of the sea almost untapped except for food for themselves. Plymouth and its bay were not suitable for a fishing fleet.

Expansion brought the Pilgrims troubles. The Dutch claimed the trading post in Connecticut. The French captured the one at Pentagoet.

The Pilgrims sent Edward Winslow to England for permission to defend themselves against these enemies. The Anglican officials thought the colonists quarrelsome and stubborn and a general nuisance. Sir Ferdinando Gorges smarted over the Pilgrims' being, in fact, squatters on land the king had granted his company and over their refusal to pay him for a license to fish in "his" waters. He proposed sending troops to New England to take over the Pilgrims' settlements and close their heretical meetinghouses.

There were several other settlements by then (1651), and they were intended for living rather than just for trading. Families had grown. New settlers kept arriving. They needed more land for crops with which to feed themselves.

People moved to Duxbury, six miles to the north, for the months of planting and harvesting, then went back to Plymouth for the winter to attend meeting and keep the colony safe. In 1632 those who had been granted lots of twenty acres along the Duxbury shore decided to stay all year. They asked to have a congregation of their own, and got a grudging permission, but it was five years before the governing body of Plymouth gave them a charter as a separate town.

Edward Winslow moved to Marshfield, and John Alden and Miles Standish to Duxbury. Towns sprang up along Cape Cod. By 1640 Plymouth Colony had eight towns with a total population of about 2500.

Life was easier for the young Saints than it had been for the *Mayflower* passengers, who now called themselves the First Comers. The new generation began to profane the sacred Sabbath day of rest by working, and—perhaps worse—they fidgeted, talked, even tittered during the meetings. Some drank, some swore, some quarreled, some wasted their time in bowling and playing "cat" (primitive baseball).

The John Alden house at Duxbury, where John and Priscilla spent their last years. It was built by their third son in 1653. By that time the Pilgrims could afford houses with more than one room.

29

Baptists and Quakers came to spread what the Saints called "horrid errors" about religion. Having been cruelly persecuted, the Pilgrims were fairly tolerant of these other heretics, and admired their courage. The Quakers made several converts in Plymouth. A few of the sons of the *Mayflower* group joined the Baptists.

The unity of the First Comers broke down. The once strong sinews of the community grew flabby through want of stretching to meet the old challenges of the land, the sea, and the weather. The colony's vigor drained away.

Their neighbors to the north, the Puritans who had begun to settle in Salem in 1628, were wiser and had greater vision and were far more aggressive. The Puritan ideals were fresh; those of Plymouth were tiring. The Puritan settlements expanded and multiplied, and their trade grew fast. The Pilgrims found themselves hemmed in.

The Puritans initiated a confederation of New England colonies against their common enemies. Plymouth signed the Articles of Confederation in September, 1643. The other colonies—Massachusetts Bay, Connecticut, and New Haven—were Puritan in spirit and government. Plymouth began to lose its identity. The sophistication of the Puritans swallowed up the simplicity of the Pilgrims.

In 1664 Samuel Maverick, an inspector of all the colonies, wrote home to England that Plymouth was "a poor small town now, the people being removed to farms in the country." The colony as a whole, Maverick added, had about twelve small towns, one iron foundry, one sawmill, no river or good harbor, no "place of strength." Poor little Plymouth suffered in contrast with the newer Puritan colonies.

Robert Cushman's sermon on greed and self-love had long been forgotten. The furious expansion of the Puritan colonies in Massachusetts and Connecticut—and, for that matter, of Plymouth to a lesser degree—led to ruthless seizure of the Indians' lands. The Indians began to see that, even when trinkets and coats and tools had been exchanged for acreage, they had lost far more than they had got. Now the English colonists were trying to convert them. To the Indians this was insult added to injury.

Massasoit, mortally sick, refused to the last to exchange his Happy Hunting Grounds for the white man's Heaven. His younger son, Metacom, had asked the Pilgrims for an English name, and had been given that of Philip. Philip eventually succeeded his older brother as chief of the Wampanoags. He had none of his father's confidence in the English. His suspiciousness was probably justified; the younger Pilgrims were undoubtedly moving into his hunting grounds in spite of the treaty Philip had renewed with the colony. Philip gathered his braves for war.

The confederated colonies summoned King Philip to conferences. By dint of their superior equipment they forced a humiliating truce on him. But for two years the truce was an open powder keg. A spark fell into it when murder was "proved" against an Indian by superstition; the corpse's wounds supposedly bled whenever the alleged assassin approached. The Indians, united under King Philip, went on the warpath.

For a year—from June, 1675, to the summer of 1676—Indians and colonists murdered one another all over New England. The warfare was equally savage and bloody on both sides. Finally Philip's supplies began to fail. His allies deserted just for the sake of food. King Philip retreated from the theater of war in western Massachusetts and Connecticut to his original home in Rhode Island.

Plymouth put Benjamin Church of Duxbury in command of a force to go after Philip. King Philip, almost completely deserted, was betrayed. He learned he was surrounded. Then he sent away his few faithful warriors and set out into the woods alone. A converted Indian shot him through the heart.

Benjamin Church cut off King Philip's head and hands, and left his quartered body for the wolves of the forest. The hands he sent to Boston. He carried the head in triumph to Plymouth and stuck it on a pike atop the new brick watch tower. It stayed there for twenty years.

King Philip's War cost Plymouth a sixth of its men. The survivors took a ruthless revenge. Captured Indians they sold into cruel slavery in the West Indies. They seized all the lands of the Wampanoags and sold them to new settlers. Even so, there was a

King Philip, as pictured by Paul Revere in the eighteenth century

staggering debt to be paid. Before Plymouth could recover completely, politics decided its fate.

The new monarchs in England—William and Mary—proved more liberal than the Stuart kings they had succeeded. The colonies petitioned them for favors. Plymouth tried to get a proper charter, but as so often happened with the Pilgrims, their plans went awry.

The Puritans' Massachusetts Bay Colony dominated the Confederation. Massachusetts learned that New York, now an English colony, had designs on Plymouth. The Puritans did not want these Anglicans from New York in New England. The Puritan agents in England had more money to spend on bribes than New York, and far more than Plymouth, which was still feebly trying to get a charter of its own.

Massachusetts slyly wrote Plymouth into the new charter it was negotiating, and got it granted in October, 1691. With the calm assurance that comes from realistic thinking, the Puritans then told the Pilgrims that their smaller colony could not defend itself against New York. Its people would be better off under the Puritans than under the Anglicans of the western colony.

In July, 1692, the governing body of Plymouth met for the last time. Its final act was to appoint the last Wednesday in August "as a day of solemn fasting and humiliation." After seventy-two years of struggle for survival, the colony of Plymouth Plantation drew its last independent breath.

Plymouth gravestone of Mrs. Mary Wait

The Pilgrims left little of practical value. None of their structures remains, and very few of their belongings. But they established the principle of free elections of governors and the making by a people of their own laws. They persuaded the Puritans to separate from the Church of England as they had done, and thus become their own masters in spiritual things. Their way of life—the congregational way, as it was called—became the basic religion of New England. And they were people who responded to a challenge with courage.

3·THE PROUD PURITANS

The Puritans came seven hundred strong in a fleet of eleven stout ships, and they had their governor with them and their charter and the firm conviction that God had appointed them to build His kingdom in the wilderness.

It was June when the *Arbella* sighted Salem. The strawberries were ripe in the meadows. Governor John Endecott of Salem,

King Charles I in a dispute with Puritans in Parliament, as pictured by John Singleton Copley

33

John Winthrop, first governor of the Massachusetts Bay Colony

whom the Puritans had sent ahead to start a trial colony, was waiting to welcome them and entertain the gentry in the "great house" he had high-handedly seized from the feeble fishing station at Gloucester.

The 350-ton *Arbella,* their flagship, with a crew of fifty-two, had sailed from Southampton and finally put to sea from Cowes on the Isle of Wight on March 29, 1630. She carried the Puritan leaders: John Winthrop, Thomas Dudley, the Reverend John Wilson, Sir Richard Saltonstall, Isaac Johnson and his wife, the Lady Arbella.

Forty-two-year-old John Winthrop was the lord of Groton Manor in Suffolk, England, a lawyer with a talent for public affairs. As a sickly student at Cambridge University he had felt God speaking directly to him out of the Bible. Thereafter, all the previous sixteen years of his life he saw as full of sin and miserable. He wept for them. Until he died in 1649, at the then advanced age of sixty-one, he strove to make up for that early blindness to God's will for him. He felt he had to find it out for himself, and alone. It was his notion of salvation.

This independence of mind brought Winthrop to the Puritans —that party of loyal members of the Church of England who wished to purify it from rituals. They distrusted the symbolism of rituals and all other religious symbols which speak through man's senses to his emotions. They believed man found the happiness they called heaven through his intelligence, not through his feelings. Such bliss was a reward for tireless intellectual effort on the part of each man to find God's will for him. Intelligence was the tool God gave man for making good use of the life God had loaned him.

Every day of his life the Puritan asked himself whether he had invested that loan wisely and increased it, or buried it, or squandered it. What might he have left undone? He was getting ready to answer the same question on that dread day when God asked it of him after his earthly days had reached their end. If God should judge His servant unworthy, God would doom him to the everlasting torments of Hell.

The seventeenth-century Puritan lived in fear of Hell as a man of the later twentieth century lives in fear of nuclear war. The Puritan pored over the Bible in search of God's will for him in order that he might come to terms with his terror. He struggled to give up himself to the total service of his divine master, and to work without stint at the tasks the Bible revealed had been set him. Laziness and self-indulgence were the Devil's sweet lures to a bitter life. Flaming Hell was the Puritan's projection of an unprofitable stay on earth.

Many Puritans in England saw that the trend of politics was making their highly individual way of life impossible. John Winthrop himself was unhappy at King Charles I's increasing autocracy. He was even more distressed at the way William Laud, Archbishop of Canterbury and head of the Church of England, was silencing Puritan preachers who did not pass his loyalty test. The Puritans wanted preaching, not rituals.

The more unhappy Puritans resolved to move to a place where they could meet in the way they agreed with one another was the right one for getting instruction in how best to do God's will for them. They formed a Company. On March 4, 1629, the Company got from King Charles a charter to plant the Massachusetts Bay Colony in an area almost the same as the present state of Massachusetts.

For his portrait, Sir Richard Saltonstall wore the new style of collar that was beginning to replace the ruff.

Six days later the king dissolved Parliament, in which the Puritans had a strong party. For all they knew, he would never call it again. Gone was their voice to limit his authority to tax them and to limit Archbishop Laud's authority over their congregations. Buried, too, was John Winthrop's talent for public affairs; the dissolution of Parliament cost him his post in the court of wards and liveries (roughly similar to our surrogate's court).

Robbed of their voice in Parliament and with their preachers being harassed, neither Winthrop nor other Puritans felt they could do God's bidding to make His Word a fact. They would be disobedient sinners, their souls eternally damned in Hell. They could already feel the bondage of Hell. Their souls were not free.

The members of the Company—substantial and contributive citizens, as were most Puritans—came to Winthrop and asked him to lead them in building a colony where they could be a free, unhampered congregation. They would call it a "city upon a hill" (Matthew 5:14), for they wanted it to be like the holy City of Zion where God himself dwelt and which was His Kingdom on earth.

Winthrop agreed, for the Company had voted to insure the colony's independence by keeping the charter and the governing body (the Great and General Court) in the colony, not in England. They elected Winthrop governor in October, 1629.

The Puritans had friends in high positions. These they persuaded—or perhaps bribed (the Puritans had plenty of money)—to hand over the charter. They owed allegiance to the king but, unlike the Pilgrims, they owed money to no man. Their colony would be completely self-governed.

Winthrop led the colonists to Charlestown at the mouth of a wide, deep harbor which rarely froze. But they found scant fresh water there, and they moved across the harbor to the treeless peninsula called Shawmut or Trimountain. On September 7, 1630, they renamed it Boston; many of them had come from Boston—St. Botolph's Town—in Lancashire, England. They settled along Boston's present Washington Street, between Milk and State Streets, near that "sweet spring" they found in what is now Spring Lane.

There in a rough field the rich built themselves houses before snow fell. The poorer settlers lived for some time in tents.

They laid out a town like an English one—a meeting house (on State Street) and a market square before it with whipping post and stocks. Nearby they raised the governor's house. Narrow lanes connected the houses. A graveyard (the one beside King's Chapel on Tremont Street) grew up on the lot of Isaac Johnson, because he wished to be buried on his own land.

That first winter some dwellings caught fire. Governor Winthrop forbade any more thatched roofs and wooden chimneys. The wood of the houses was green and soon warped. Pigs roamed and rooted in the mud of the lanes. The meeting house was bare and cheerless. It was a dreary "city upon a hill."

Four years later, the colonists bought forty-five acres of land from the hermit William Blackstone, the only white man they had found in Shawmut, who lived at the corner of present Beacon and

Spruce Streets. These acres they set apart for "common use"—for cattle to graze on, and drink from the pond, as they still may legally do on Boston Common.

Except for the Common and its Frog Pond and the gravestones, nothing remains of the Boston the early Puritans built. What stayed was the New England Way by which John Winthrop and his people lived.

They agreed with one another on this Way. Their agreement was a holy covenant. They desired "not to vary from the doctrine of faith and truth held forth by the churches of their native country." But they disliked the word Church. Each congregation made its own rules and called its own minister to preach in its meetinghouse.

There they listened to long and learned sermons addressed to their intelligence, each man hoping to find some proof in them that God's Word spoke straight to him. Then, to the preachers who examined him, he could give evidence that he had been truly converted. They would make him a full member of the congregation, and then he could cast a vote for the governor and the magistrates.

Their "city upon a hill" was a home they were building at a sacrifice and with hard toil. They meant to do as they wanted in it—welcome some guests, shut others out. Differences of opinion, criticism of their Way, offended them as a group, much as contradiction or adverse comment insulted any one of them in his own house. God's purposes were clear in the Bible. There neither was nor could be any other authority.

The Puritans knew who they were and where they were going. Those who disagreed were not only unwanted but of unsound judgment, hence dangerous.

Brilliant young Roger Williams arrived on the *Lyon* in February, 1631, and later was called to the ministry of the Salem congregation. Soon he protested against the New England Way. But Governor Winthrop thought him a "godly minister," even when Williams questioned the General Court's right to powers they saw clearly granted them in the Bible.

John Cotton and Thomas Hooker, ministers who had urged

Silver communion cup presented to Boston's First Church by Governor Winthrop. He obtained it in London, where it was made in 1610.

Williams to come to New England, labored with him but "could not reduce him from any of his errors." These included Williams' opinion that the colonists had stolen their land from the Indians, and so their charter was sinful. The General Court judged the Salem minister not only heretical but treasonous.

The Court gave the young genius time to repent, for Governor Winthrop saw how useful he could be to the colony. Williams refused to change his convictions. Few if any Puritans ever did. The Court banished him on October 9, 1635.

Roger Williams went to his Indian friends on Aquidneck Island (the actual island of Rhode Island) and lived for the rest of the winter in their filthy, smoky huts. In April, 1636, he bought new land from them and began to plant the colony of Providence at the head of Narragansett Bay. There no man was to be "molested for his conscience."

Anne Hutchinson was a witty woman, forty-three years old when the *Griffin* landed at Boston in 1634, and the mother of several children including a grown son. Her husband William was known as stupid and mild-tempered, but Anne was a skillful nurse and midwife, and generous with her services, and other women adored her.

Anne moved into the big house William Hutchinson built diagonally opposite Governer Winthrop's and began to improve Boston. She had hated it as soon as she saw it from the ship; she almost went back to England on the *Griffin*.

Mistress Anne invited the women of Boston to her fine house and gave them interpretations of the sermons of dull John Wilson, whom she loathed, and of the teaching of eloquent John Cotton, whom she loved. Soon she was claiming that she could prophesy. And she maintained that revelation came straight from God, not through the Bible or any creed, and that anyone who had such revelation could do as he wished.

To the Puritan women who had no rights whatever and no diversions, Anne Hutchinson was freedom and independence in the flesh. One Boston dame saucily told Captain Edward Johnson of the militia: "Come along with me, and I'll bring you to a woman who preaches better gospel than any of your black coats that have

A sachem of the Narragansett Indians of Rhode Island, wearing a summer costume of buckskin. His necklace and headgear were made of shells.

been at the ninny-versity."

Anne went too far. She attacked the Reverend John Wilson's opinions. The General Court summoned her before them in November, 1637. She had her partisans, but she had a mortal enemy in Governor John Winthrop. Winthrop had had three wives and was convinced that women's intelligence was weak. He did not like a meddling woman.

Anne Hutchinson stood sick and shivering with cold in the draughty meetinghouse while the Court tried her "for traducing the ministers and their ministry." She defended herself well, until she talked too much about her revelations and so sealed her doom.

The Court banished her. Anne and her family followed Roger Williams to Aquidneck, where her husband died. Then she moved herself and her family to New York. Indians killed her in 1643.

When the Quakers "felt moved" to go to Boston to preach their convictions, not too different from Anne Hutchinson's, they were whipped, had their ears cut off, and were banished. The stubborn were hanged. They tempted the Puritans to make them martyrs, but the Puritans did not like to dignify the interfering Quakers with that reward. The magistrates pleaded long and hard with Mary Dyer to stop her preaching and accept banishment, but she kept coming back; and at last they had to hang her on Boston Common.

The Puritans were fanatically single-minded about defending the unity of their "city upon a hill." Present protection, however, was not enough. They looked also to the future. That lay in training the intelligence of the young who would come after them.

The leaders had trained their own intelligence in the colleges of Cambridge in England. Their sons could not follow them there. They would have to have a college of their own.

Possibly the most famous words of the Puritans—and they wrote millions—are the ones in which they told of the founding of Harvard College in October, 1636:

> After God had carried us safe to New England, and we had builded
> our houses, provided necessaries for our livelihood, reared convenient
> places for God's worship, and settled the civil government, one of the
> next things we longed for and looked after was to advance learning

and perpetuate it to posterity, dreading to leave an illiterate ministry to the churches when our present ministers shall lie in the dust. And as we were thinking and consulting how to effect this great work, it pleased God to stir up the heart of one Mr. Harvard (a godly gentleman and a lover of learning, there living amongst us) to give the one half of his estate (it being in all about £. 1700) towards the erecting of a college, and all his library. After him, another gave £. 300. Others after them cast in more, and the public hand of the state added the rest. The college was, by common consent, appointed to be at Cambridge (a place very pleasant and accommodate) and is called (according to the name of its first founder) Harvard College.

In the same year the General Court started an endowed school in Boston. Salem did the same in 1639. Roxbury's Latin School has functioned since its founding in 1645. Two years later the Court ruled that every town of fifty households or more must provide a free elementary school.

For the first time in history a government had offered free education to all its boys. Free education, and the freedom education brings, are an ancient part of the New England Way.

The colony thrived. It was the first in America to prosper. Since many of the colonists were joint stockholders in the Massachusetts Bay Company, they profited as individuals.

There was a steady market in Europe for the fish and lumber available to the colonists in extravagant plenty just for the catching or cutting. There were grassy meadows for raising farm animals to sell abroad, and acres of easily grown corn to ship for their fodder. Land was free for the taking and tilling. Opportunity stretched as wide as the sea, and the sea was all that lay between an enterprising man's ill luck in old England and a fortune in New England.

In England, King Charles I, with no Parliament to limit his power, was levying heavier and heavier taxes. Refugees from the Thirty Years' War on the Continent streamed into England and depressed the labor market. Economic disaster loomed for businessmen, tradesmen, and skilled workers.

New colonists poured into Massachusetts Bay and spread out from the harbors and cleared the land and built new settlements. By 1640 the colony had some twenty thousand inhabitants and

Many generations of New Englanders learned the alphabet from the New England Primer, *first published in 1689 by a Boston bookseller.*

In *Adam's* Fall
We Sinned all.

Thy Life to Mend
This *Book* Attend.

The *Cat* doth play
And after slay.

twenty-eight thriving towns besides Boston. Some, like agricultural Springfield and Longmeadow, were far inland. Others, like Marblehead on the coast near Salem, were for fishing.

The property owners in these towns would meet informally to air quarrels that arose in their community. These they had to refer to the General Court for a ruling. But they found that the General Court—the governor, his deputy, and six assistants—was too small to deal adequately with the individual problems of so many towns. Consequently the townsmen demanded the right to send to the General Court two representatives from each town, who would present their problems and share in making laws to settle them. These delegates made a lower house in the General Court. They soon got for the towns the right to choose their own officials for handling the local problems which kept increasing as the towns grew in size.

The early informal meetings soon became regularly scheduled ones, at first for every month, later for every year. A town meeting began with prayers led by the minister of the local congregation. Then a moderator was elected by the property owners, and a clerk to keep minutes. A "warrant," or agenda, was discussed according to parliamentary procedure. The voters then elected selectmen—that is, "chosen men"—to deal with town matters between meetings. As community life got more intricate, the property owners also elected constables, clerks, surveyors, a school board, and other department heads. All these officials were subject to the voters' audit at the next town meeting.

The institution and the procedure of the town meeting became the basis of constitutional government in America. The town meeting made the people politically aware. It taught them to control and limit the authority by which they consented to be governed, whether at home or from England. Each town was a miniature republic.

In England, authority was already so out of control that the Puritans who had stayed at home rebelled against their autocratic king. By 1642 there was civil war between their forces.

The war put an end to the stream of immigrants. Some colonists went back to England to join one side or the other. The war also

D

A *Dog* will bite
A Thief at night.

E

An *Eagles* flight
Is out of fight.

F

The Idle *Fool*
Is whipt at School.

A room from an Ipswich house about 1640. The Puritans could generally afford more elaborate furniture than the Pilgrims.

ended New England's first boom times. The people could not get the commodities they needed from England, principally iron for farming implements or the tools themselves. The value of their own agricultural products dropped to nothing. England could get these from her own people or from the Baltic.

The colonists who had kept their eyes on the land turned around and saw the sea, over which they had entered, as a life-saving exit from the crisis. Much nearer than England lay the islands of the West Indies, where slave labor produced tons of sugar cane for export in one form or another, but nothing for the islands' subsistence. All necessities had to be imported.

New Englanders took to the sea.

Fishing and trade and the building of ships and the sailing of them beckoned young men from the back-breaking work of clearing trees and boulders off land that, even when open, had already proved to have sparse soil. Youngsters of twelve stole off, to return as respected captains at twenty to build their own ships and reap the profits. The sea with its own riches and its easy way to others would be the prime source of New England's wealth and power for two centuries to come.

The change fixed the whole growth of the region. New settlements sprang up only on the coast or on rivers with easy access to the sea. For there were yet no roads worthy of the name from the ports to the farms. The inland farmer, who was rarely farther than thirty miles from the tides, prospered only when he could get his products and his by-products to the ships.

Huge areas stayed wild for a hundred years. Most of the vast region which would become the states of New Hampshire and Vermont was not even explored, much less surveyed, for another hundred years. As late as 1713 there were only seven settlements in New Hampshire. But coastal settlements thrived on fishing and shipbuilding. England's Navigation Acts, which forced the colonists to ship their exports in English-made boats, stimulated shipbuilding, in Maine as well as Massachusetts and Rhode Island.

The Pine Tree Shilling of "Masathusets" was the first silver coin made in New England. Coins from several European nations continued to circulate also.

The founders had hoped to keep their Massachusetts Bay Colony a unit in politics and religion. But the Puritans themselves were fierce individuals, too independent to compromise their freedom. Each man and each congregation had to find their own way of meeting their needs, whether for land to support their bodies or for principles to feed their souls. Their religion had made them so.

Indians from the west kept visiting Boston, bringing good reports of land along the Connecticut River. Roger Ludlow of crowded Dorchester heeded them. In 1635 he led a migration to Windsor to settle near the trading post the Pilgrims had developed. Richard Denton and John Sherman left Watertown and founded Wethersfield in the same year.

These settlers were squatters on land the English king had granted to a group of noblemen under the Warwick Patent. A patent was a right to a settlement; it was not a charter. The Dutch also claimed the land, and had begun to settle it for the sake of trading for furs with the Indians.

Governor Winthrop's son John was too strong-minded and too intelligent—he had a great talent for science and medicine—to stay

under his able father's firm authority. In 1634 he went from Boston to England and got permission from the grantees of the Warwick Patent to found a colony on their land. In November, 1635, he sent twenty men to the mouth of the Connecticut River. They tore down the Dutch fort there and built houses. The following spring Winthrop himself came, and named the place Saybrook—after the two English noblemen who had the patent, Lord Brooke and Lord Say and Sele.

Thomas Hooker landed at Boston in 1633 and went to his waiting congregation in well-settled Newtowne (Cambridge). Within a year he was disputing matters of religion with his friend and former shipmate on the *Griffin,* John Cotton. Cotton was the teacher of the Boston congregation; that is, he explained doctrine, whereas the preacher urged his flock to make real their faith in good works.

New England in 1677, with west (and the Connecticut River) at the top. This woodcut map was made by John Foster, a young Cambridge printer. He numbered the towns that had been "assaulted by the Indians."

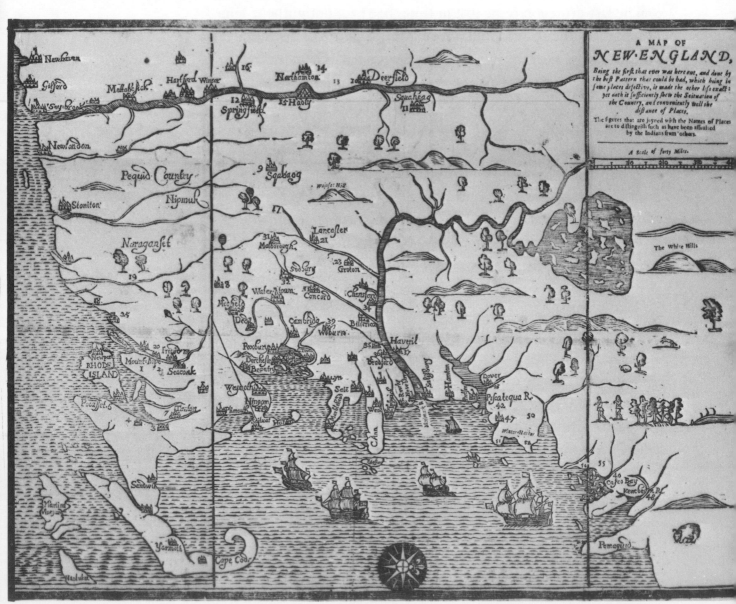

Hooker and a hundred of his people walked over Indian trails through the virgin forest, driving their cattle before them, and founded Hartford on the Connecticut River in 1636.

John Winthrop, Jr., declared all the land of the Warwick Patent a separate colony, outside the law of the Massachusetts Bay Colony. He persuaded Hooker and the other squatters to his independent point of view, and they elected him governor of the small area (about 5000 square miles) after Winthrop had confirmed their rights to their settlements. The new colony was called Connecticut.

Winthrop appealed to the Massachusetts General Court to arbitrate the issue of whether or not the new colony could have an independent government. The Warwick Patent did not make this important matter clear. The Massachusetts General Court decided that, yes, a body of eight men might set up a General Court for the new colony, to make decrees, and even wage war.

The last provision came just in time. In 1637, not without some provocation, the Pequot Indians went on the warpath, determined to exterminate the white usurpers of their lands. The new General Court of Connecticut, which met at Hartford, ordered an offensive war against the Pequots, raised an army of ninety men, and named Captain John Mason its commander.

Mason trapped the Pequots in their own stockade at Mystic, set it afire and burned up most of the Indian men, women, and children inside. The few who broke out were killed. Only seven escaped. Between six and seven hundred perished.

With the help of Captain Israel Stoughton and his 120 men from Massachusetts, Mason pursued the rest of the Pequots and slaughtered or captured all but some two hundred of them. These surrendered themselves and their land. "Thus," wrote Mason at the end of his history of the war, "the Lord was pleased to smite our enemies in the hinder parts, and to give us their land for an inheritance."

Captain Stoughton went back to Boston enthusiastic about the possibilities for a settlement at the mouth of the Quinnipiac River, where there was a fine harbor. "Get there before the Dutch do," he urged.

John Davenport and Theophilus Eaton had just arrived with a

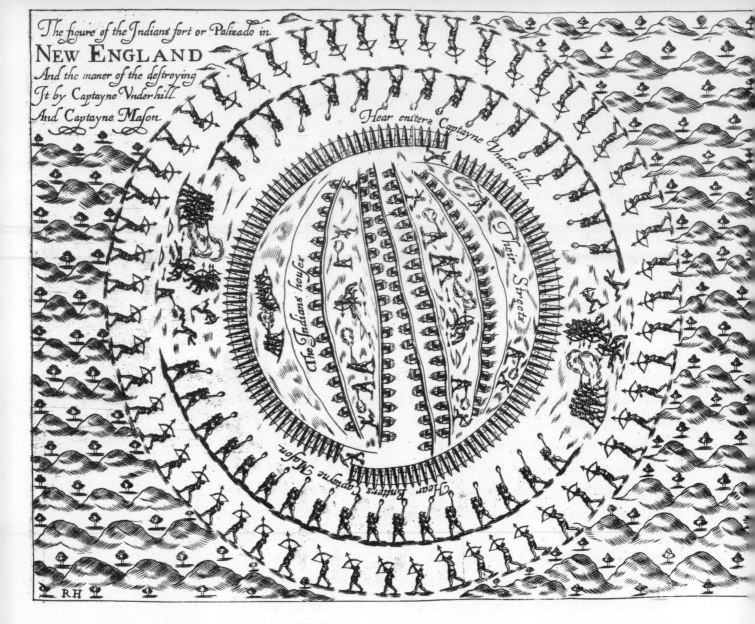

Within the illustration:

The figure of the Indians fort or Palizado in
NEW ENGLAND
And the maner of the destroying
It by Captayne Vnderhill
And Captayne Mason.

Hear ent'era Captayne Vnderhill

The Indians houses

Their Streets

Hear enters Captayne Mason

RH

*The massacre of Pequot
Indians at Mystic, as described
by Captain Mason
and pictured in a book
published in 1638*

sizable group of their English parishioners and friends. All were devoutly eager to establish a "Bible State" in New England. They were rich and they were staunch Puritans of the strictest variety. They found nothing to please them in Boston, neither a site for a colony nor religion to their liking. The trial of Anne Hutchinson and the protests of her followers indicated to them that there was mutiny in the ranks of those they had thought solidly faithful to the Puritan covenant.

The Quinnipiac region seemed God's destination for the Davenport-Eaton company. Eaton inspected it and reported it good. The congregation set sail from Boston on March 30, 1638, and landed on April 14, and named the place Quinnipiac. (They renamed it New Haven in 1640.) That first summer they laid out the famous New Haven Green.

The weakened, frightened Indians sold them a tract of land along the shore. This extended to Stamford on the west, to Milford on the east, and as far inland as Meriden. The newcomers made it a separate colony and drew up a constitution based on the law of Moses as interpreted by John Davenport, the first governor. The government was completely in the hands of the church. Trial by jury did not exist, nor any other privileges guaranteed the individual under English common law. Punishments were cruel.

The New Haven colonists wanted a college, and in 1648 they named a committee to look into building one "so soon as their ability will reach thereunto." It was fifty-three more years, however, before anything concrete was done. Meanwhile John Davenport, worn out with the religious and financial and political problems of his colony, had gone back to die in Massachusetts. By then the more sophisticated and more democratic Connecticut Colony had, in 1664, absorbed New Haven.

John Davenport, first governor of the New Haven Colony. This painting by John Foster is one of the earliest portraits painted in New England.

After Mason's defeat of the Pequots in 1637, the towns of Connecticut grew rapidly. The major threat of the Indians seemed gone, though there would still be plenty of isolated Indian raids and massacres in the Connecticut River valley for years to come. As the towns grew, so did their problems. It became clear to the "planters" that they needed a basic law.

In January, 1639, they met in Hartford and adopted the eleven Fundamental Orders of Connecticut, one of the world's first written constitutions for a government. They were based on the heart of a sermon Thomas Hooker had preached the previous May 31, namely, that it is the people's right to elect their officers and to limit their power. The preamble of the Orders states that "there should be an orderly and decent government established . . . to order and dispose of the affairs of the people."

The unity of spirit the Boston Puritans so much desired in their commonwealth was strong in Connecticut but not in Rhode Island. In 1638 two hundred believers in Anne Hutchinson's theory of revelation left Boston to found Portsmouth on Aquidneck Island. The following year, William Coddington and some thirty others broke away—they quarreled with Anne Hutchinson—and founded Newport.

Coddington had been the treasurer of the Massachusetts Bay Company and one of the richest men in Boston. His associates had been prominent men in England. They were all broad-minded, outstanding politically and socially. In Newport they separated church and state and set up a conservative, orderly government.

Their tradition of wealth and their ability for commercial enterprise made Newport prosper. It had a fine natural harbor and inland resources of timber and farm land. By 1680 it led the colonies, along with Boston, in shipbuilding. And from the very beginning it had a tradition of large estates; Coddington's own was one thousand acres.

Roger Williams sailed for England to get a charter for Rhode Island. It was granted on March 24, 1644. The settlements of Portsmouth, Newport, and Warwick joined with Providence to become a single colony. Warwick had been founded in 1643 by Samuel Gorton, who had been banished from Boston for maintaining that Christ was both human and divine, and that heaven and hell are imaginary places. Roger Williams was elected chief officer of Rhode Island's democratic government.

The Massachusetts towns, and later the Connecticut ones, were laid out as a symbol of the close connection between church and state. The ministers of the churches were not actually officials of the government, but they might as well have been, so great was their influence. The towns were planned around a "green"; meetinghouse, school, Town House (City Hall) rose simultaneously with the houses.

In Rhode Island the towns were settled not by ministers but by stubbornly independent laymen. The towns grew casually, along the boundaries of the land grants. The coastline also determined their shape. There were water lots and upland meadows.

In Newport, for example, the main street ran along the shore of Narragansett Bay. The structures—wharves, water mills, tar pits for the ships—rose where they were needed. Choice lots in the center of town were set aside to attract tradesmen.

In all the colonies the houses were much alike, built by local carpenters ignorant of how architecture was developing in England under such masters of the baroque style as Inigo Jones, Christopher Wren, and John Vanbrugh. The colonial structures were still like those of the Middle Ages in Europe.

The houses rest on stone foundations. Generally their walls are of board, sometimes painted with red earth or lampblack. Brick was not much used until after 1700. The windows are small, with rectangular or diamond-shaped panes of glass, for warmth and cheapness. (Sometimes oiled paper substituted for glass.)

Inside, the walls were plastered or sheathed with tongue-and-groove boards for warmth. The floors were sanded. The massive furniture consisted of trestle tables, benches, chests or cupboards; beds were sometimes built into the walls.

With alarm, the Bay Colony saw its strength scattered. The Civil War in England might induce the French or the Dutch—not to mention the Indians—to attack the colonies England was helpless to defend. The Boston magistrates invited the colonies of Plymouth, Connecticut, and New Haven to make an alliance for

Boston's first Town House, drawn by a modern artist from the original plans of 1657. Above an open market space were the meeting rooms of the General Court. At left are the pillory and the whipping post. After this wooden building burned down in 1711, it was replaced on the same site by the beautiful brick Town House known today as the Old State House (page 90).

For warmth, early New England houses had large central chimneys and small windows. This house (1692) is in Wethersfield, Connecticut.

"their mutual safety and welfare." Rhode Island was not asked to join; the Massachusetts Puritans had no wish to associate with its heretics. Maine and New Hampshire were ineligible for membership; they were still the personal property of Sir Ferdinando Gorges, a loyal supporter of King Charles I against the Puritan party in England.

Articles of Confederation were agreed upon in 1643, establishing the United Colonies of New England. Then Massachusetts, the largest and richest of the colonies, began to lead and dominate the union and to spread its influence over the members as it would continue to do for more than a century.

Secure again, the Bay Colony undertook at last the fulfillment of its charter, which stated that "the principle end of this plantation" was to convert the Indians to the Christian faith. The Puritans had neglected this objective on the excuse that the Indian language was too great a stumbling block.

John Eliot, the gentle, winning minister of the Roxbury congregation, saw his calling to break the barrier. One of the Pequot War captives was given him as a slave. From this Indian, whom he later set free, Eliot learned the Algonquin language. He then could preach the gospel to the heathen in their own tongue.

Eliot simplified the intricate beliefs of the Puritans—so complicated that today it is impossible to say exactly what their faith as a whole was—to the teachings of the first Christians: repentance, prayer, fellowship in the spirit. This approach to religion got him into some trouble with the Puritan authorities, but along with his own kind and generous and tireless labors, it won him some converts.

What success Eliot had as a missionary came largely from his knack for adapting Puritan standards to the customs of the Indians. Also he could see that turning a converted Indian loose in the wilderness would only turn him back into a heathen. So he established some fourteen "Praying Villages" in which his redeemed Indians could live together and keep their new faith pure. Then, to strengthen and expand their faith, he spent eight years translating the Bible into Algonquin, and taught his converts to read it. Read it they did after it had been printed in 1663, for some of their well-thumbed copies of this "Mamusse wanneetupanatamme up-biblum God" exist today.

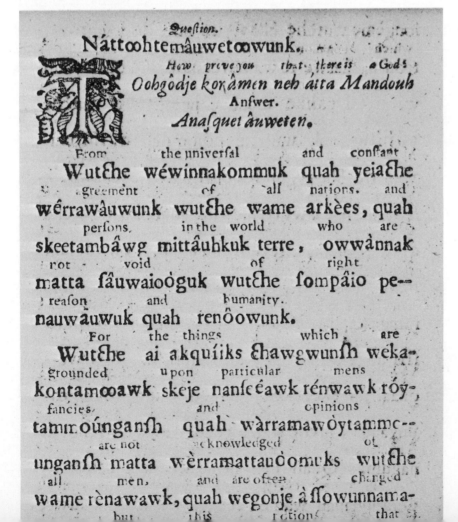

This religious book was printed in Algonquin with an English translation.

On the Massachusetts Bay Colony seal, an Indian asked the settlers for help.

Eliot's Praying Indians and their Praying Villages, however good in intention, nevertheless brought woe to the colonies. They were one of the causes of King Philip's War. King Philip resented the invasion of his people's minds as seriously as he did the white man's encroachments on their lands.

The death and devastation of the war was a terrible shock to all New Englanders, particularly to the people of Massachusetts. For over fifty years they had had peace and prosperity. They had lived on good terms with the Indians, had even done them the great favor of converting them to Christianity. What had gone wrong? There was much searching of heart as the Puritans wept over the graves of their dead and the bleak ruins of their towns. Had their God forsaken them?

The first generation of Puritans were gone to their reward. The younger ones, now in command, were not the men their fathers were. But they felt there must be a return to the old strength, the independence of spirit, the uncompromising enforcement of the principles which had set them apart as the people God had chosen to found and maintain His kingdom on earth.

The new generation forgot that the founders were careful planners and had a shrewd sense of timing. The younger leaders acted abruptly and took no account of the strength of their opponents. "The laws of England," declared Governor Leverett of Massachusetts, "do not apply here." The colonists flouted England's trade laws, suppressed the Church of England, denied Englishmen their legal rights. This defiance of the mother country seemed to them a justifiable preservation of their chosen way.

Slowly but effectively England retaliated. In 1684, King Charles II voided the charter of Massachusetts. His successor, King James II, two years later sent Sir Edmund Andros—who had been recalled to England for tyranically mismanaging New York Colony —to be Massachusetts' governor.

Andros was technically the governor of all the New England colonies. But when he demanded the Connecticut charter, the colonists hid it, supposedly in an oak tree, and he never got around to grabbing Rhode Island's. Massachusetts was the theater for his acts of tyranny.

Andros seized Boston's Old South Meetinghouse for the Anglican services the Puritans hated. He levied poll taxes and property taxes. He declared that all land titles had been voided along with the charter. He imprisoned John Wise, the minister of Ipswich, for declaring that taxation without representation was tyranny. When Wise demanded rights under English law, Andros replied: "Mr. Wise, you have no more privileges left you than not to be sold for slaves."

There are very few American portraits of women and children from the seventeenth century. This painting shows Mrs. Mary Freake and her baby, both in their best clothes (about 1674).

Young Cotton Mather had graduated from Harvard and become the colleague of his father at Boston's Second Church. He was the grandson of Reverend John Cotton and of Reverend Richard Mather, who compiled the *Bay Psalm Book*, the first book published in America. Cotton Mather's father, the Reverend Increase Mather, was president of Harvard College and the colony's ambassador to England. Cotton Mather, who would be the foremost Puritan of his day, was intellectually brilliant and incredibly learned, and he had an extremely complex personality.

Richard Mather, a woodcut portrait by John Foster, who also made the woodcut map on page 44.

Cotton Mather's first public service in a long lifetime of consecration to public affairs was to read from the balcony of Boston's Town House a declaration of rebellion against Sir Edmund Andros. The colonists shipped Andros back to England in 1689.

Increase Mather was in London, trying to get the Massachusetts charter restored, when he learned of this rebellion, which his son had instigated. By explaining it away with his considerable talent for diplomacy, he managed to get a new charter confirming many of the old liberties and the land titles. But the right of the colony to elect its own governor was gone forever.

Massachusetts had to accept this charter in 1692. No colony could survive without England's protection against the French in Canada, who were already stirring up the Indians against the English. A century of war had begun in Europe, to be waged chiefly between England and France, for the balance of power in the whole western world.

Cotton Mather interpreted the humiliation of Massachusetts as a penalty for the religious backsliding of the colony. From his pulpit he thundered that Satan had been loosed from bondage and was seeking to destroy the "city upon a hill" as a punishment for its wickedness. Mather's presentation of the evidence was eloquent and stirring. The people became hysterical with guilt.

How else could they account for what had gone wrong—the horrible war, the injustice of Andros, the loss of their sacred liberty to choose their governor? Something evil must be at work, invisible, intangible, but not nameless. Its name was the Devil, and it was all the more to be feared because it could not be seen or touched or perceived except in the mind. The hysterical people became panicky with fear.

The Puritans quailed as they saw their ruthlessness staring back at them from the mirror of conscience they expected to reflect their righteousness: the burning of the Pequot Indians; the hanging of the Quakers; the banishment into the cruel winter of Roger Williams and Anne Hutchinson. They could not endure this image of themselves. The mirror was the Devil's looking glass. Smash it and destroy the hideous image they could not face!

So when two bored, unloved little girls in the household of the minister of Salem Village (Danvers) started screaming at their black slave Tituba, and shrieking—after they had got the attention they wanted—that they were bewitched, the Puritans at last had evidence of the Devil and his work through human beings who had given him power over them. He could be destroyed by destroying his creatures.

But Tituba had loved the girls and petted them and told them by the firelight tales of Voodoo rites in her native Carib island. The girls brought their lonely chums to hear her. It occurred to them that they could brighten up the dreary winter of 1692-93 by acting out the fantasies the simple-minded slave had created for them.

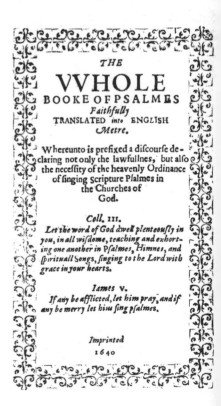

Title page of the first edition of Mather's Bay Psalm Book.

As child actors they were utterly convincing, especially to an audience that wanted to be convinced. The girls were believed when they pointed at poor old women and village half-wits and cantankerous old men whom nobody liked anyway, and fell into convulsions, and shouted that the perverted souls of these derelicts were torturing them in the shape of a yellow bird up there on the rafters.

The lordly magistrates who were summoned from Boston, and Cotton Mather, who was called because he was so learned that he must know all the wiles of the Devil, half saw the yellow bird themselves. "Thou shalt not suffer a witch to live," said the Book of Exodus in an obscure phrase that Cotton Mather discovered. There was their authority and their directive. Besides, witches had been found in Connecticut, and they had been hanged.

And so on Gallows Hill in Salem, nineteen men and women were hanged, and one man was pressed to death by a millstone for refusing to answer the charges of witchcraft against him. For how could a man reply to the accusation that not he himself had tortured a child but had sent his spirit to pinch and pull her?

The new royal governor, Sir William Phips, put an end to the witch trials and released from prison the 150 men and women accused of being in league with the Devil. But the bodies dangling on the gibbet haunted at least one of the magistrates who had set them writhing there.

Judge Samuel Sewall, whose skill at cross-examination had trapped the defendants at their trial for witchcraft, sat on Christmas Eve five years later, hearing his son read from the Gospel according to St. Matthew: "If ye had known what this meaneth, 'I will have mercy and not sacrifice,' ye would not have condemned the guiltless." Christ seemed to speak to him directly, as Judge Sewall had hoped He might, though not with such a sharp rebuke.

Judge Sewall wrote out a confession that he had acted in error, repented, and wished to take on himself "the blame and shame of it." He stood with bowed head for all to see while his confession was read in the meetinghouse.

On the same day the jurors at the witch trials who had not dared defy the judges' charges begged forgiveness. So, one by one, did many of those who had given testimony. Finally, ten years later, Ann Putnam, who had started all the dreadful mischief, with streaming tears repented and was forgiven.

But the pride of the Puritans lay in the dust. And New England had to turn its energies to fending off a far more real and visible enemy than the Devil.

Judge Samuel Sewall. This painting is by John Smibert, one of a long line of gifted portrait painters in New England.

4·THE ROAD TO REBELLION

The frontier village of Salmon Falls, thirteen miles north of Portsmouth, New Hampshire, awoke on March 18, 1690, to find the forest behind it alive. But its rustlings were not of spring. Out swept a whooping band of fifty creatures—half Frenchified Indians, half Indianized French. They broke into the stockade at two places. They broke into the fort. They killed thirty-four of the villagers, and carried off fifty-four.

In Europe, Catholic Louis XIV of France had gone to war with Protestant William III of England in an effort to extend France's frontier to the Rhine and, incidentally, to restore Catholic James II

Boston's Liberty Tree

57

to the throne of England, from which his Protestant subjects had chased him.

King William's War, which earlier that year had brought similar raids on the Hudson River towns of New York and other frontier areas, now would harass New England. To the New Englanders' ancient foes, the Indians, were added the French.

The New Englanders hated the French because the French were Catholics. They despised the French, who married Indians and adopted many of their customs. They envied the ease with which the French converted the Indians. All Canada was French, including its eastern islands, which menaced the New England coast.

Now the French had allied themselves with the Indians and so had a long arm to reach into New England and claw at settlements not far from Boston itself. And French privateers from the French naval base at Port Royal, Nova Scotia, were capturing New England ships in New England waters.

Now Massachusetts had justification for an attack on Port Royal.

William Phips was a Maine boy from Pemaquid, where he had learned shipbuilding. He had worked at this trade in Boston. He was prospering as a shipbuilding contractor and merchant captain when he heard of sunken Spanish treasure ships off the Bahamas. One expedition he equipped to salvage them failed, but the next one raised a galleon off Haiti. Phips's share of the loot came to sixteen thousand pounds (about $800,000). The share that went to the British crown got Phips a knighthood from grateful King James II.

Returning to Boston with his new wealth and title, Sir William Phips ingratiated himself with the powerful Mathers. They got him command of an expedition against Port Royal.

It took Phips only three weeks in May, 1690, to sail to Port Royal with seven hundred men in fourteen ships, force the base to surrender, plunder it, and sail back to Boston with prisoners and booty. Phips was now a hero.

The French retaliated with a massacre at Casco (Falmouth, Maine) and the capture of Portland.

Massachusetts then sent Phips with two thousand men and thirty-four ships to Quebec. This move was supposed to be part of a general colonial offensive against Canada. The expedition was a dismal failure. Phips was largely to blame, but the Mathers proclaimed from their pulpit that the disaster was a judgment of God on the sinful people of the "city upon a hill." Phips went on under Mather patronage to become governor of the colony.

The Quebec expedition cost the colony over two and a half million dollars which it did not have. To pay off the clamoring soldiers and sailors, it issued paper money and levied heavy taxes to make it good.

King William's War dragged on for another six years of French-Indian raids on New England towns and retaliations by New Englanders. Most of the latter were led by the same blustering Benjamin Church who had sent King Philip's hands to Boston. But the most conspicuous single maneuver was the work of Mrs. Hannah Dustin.

On March 15, 1697, Hannah Dustin was recovering from the birth of her eighth child when the Abenakis descended on her farm community near Haverhill, Massachusetts. Her husband was in his fields with their seven other children. He sent them running to a fortified house. He started to rescue his wife. The Indians got between him and the house. All he could do was retreat and keep firing to give his children time to reach shelter. The savages carried off Hannah Dustin, her week-old infant, and her nurse Mary Neff.

The Indians bashed the squalling baby's brains out against a tree.

For six weeks the Abenakis drove the two women and a neighbor boy northward through the forest until they were near their own home village. There, the Indians said, they would strip the women naked and make them run the gauntlet. Hannah Dustin decided to make a break for freedom.

While the Indians lay snoring around a dying fire, she roused Mary Neff and the boy. Noiselessly they found hatchets and systematically killed their captors.

Hannah had all the thrift typical of a New England housewife. She knew there was a bounty for a dead Indian. She waited until

The Mathers were among New England's most influential families. Increase Mather (above) served as the Massachusetts Bay Colony's ambassador to England. His son Cotton Mather (below) was considered the foremost Puritan of his day.

dawn gave her light enough to see, then scalped her victims, and started back to Haverhill with her hairy trophies.

Massachusetts paid her fifty pounds for the scalps, and Hannah Dustin rejoined her husband and children.

When a peace treaty was signed at Ryswick, Holland, on September 30, 1697, England had checked Louis XIV's ambitions in Europe, but the French empire in North America remained unsurrendered and unchanged. Much, however, changed in New England.

Sir William Phips was only one example of how a poor country boy could become a millionaire and the most important man in his

Boston harbor with Castle William, built in 1704. Paul Revere, who made this print, included several small boats as well as a British warship. Until the Revolution, the British flag flew everywhere in New England.

community. John Hull, the greatest Boston merchant of the time, was the barely educated son of a blacksmith; he died worth over six thousand pounds after having occasionally advanced money to the colony's treasury out of his own funds. Abraham Lincoln's great-great-great-grandfather Mordecai, the son of an indentured servant, was a blacksmith's apprentice who saved to buy a waterfall in Cohasset. There he built a mill and a forge, worked them hard, and died a rich man.

Wealth brought new names into the register of Boston's worthies: Jeremiah Dummer, Peter Faneuil, Samuel Belcher, Thomas Hancock—all of whom had started life as poor apprentices. In New England a man was not bound to one craft and to one class of society as he had been in the apprentice-guild system of Europe. Furthermore, New England's variety of economic opportunity—agriculture, seamanship, commerce—meant that an enterprising youth could be a jack-of-all-trades and thus increase his earning capacity. The new sin was failure to take advantage of the social revolution.

The older Puritans' faith was that God rewarded a man for hard work at the calling He assigned him with admission to heaven. That was the Puritan ethic. It was valid when the first settlers lived in unity of principle and in simplicity. But the later generations had got involved in fishing and trade and shipbuilding and colonizing—not so unified or so simple as clearing the wilderness and raising corn. Now God seemed to be rewarding His hard-working people with massacres and wars and paper money and high taxes.

The ministers had to change their tune. Calling on the people to repent was no way to control the dictatorship of a non-elected governor or stave off French-Indian raids.

None was more realistic than Cotton Mather. He saw that for religion to survive, ill-paid ministers should stop preaching the virtues of poverty and the sinfulness of wealth to congregations who could buy power and were building stately edifices.

The Puritan ethic changed into the Protestant ethic. Its difference is that a man has himself—and luck—to thank for his material success. He looks to God for guidance in using it in public service and for the benefit of less well-rewarded human beings. The

Peter Faneuil, a portrait by John Smibert. Faneuil provided the funds for Boston's original Faneuil Hall, designed by Smibert and built in 1742. The building, which was enlarged by Charles Bulfinch in 1805, is still in use.

This painted pine box from Deerfield (eighteenth century) shows the Indians attacking the settlers with tomahawks.

Protestant ethic, the spirit of capitalism, was a new milestone along the New England Way.

During King William's War, England had sent only four companies of soldiers to fight her enemies in North America. The colonies were thought to have both men and money enough to protect themselves. Queen Anne's War followed King William's War. England stayed indifferent to the colonists' appeals for help against disasters like the Deerfield massacre of February 29, 1704.

The 270 inhabitants of that frontier town were asleep when 200 Canadians and 140 Indians fell upon them. Many of the settlers escaped death, but 38 were killed and 111 prisoners were marched three hundred miles north to Montreal.

The Reverend John Williams wrote a book about the experiences of his own family on this death march. His infant son was killed at the outset. Two days later his wife fainted from exhaustion as she trudged through a blizzard. An Indian brained her with his tomahawk. Their Negro slave was also killed. Williams was ransomed, but his 10-year-old daughter Eunice remained with the Indians. She married a converted Indian and stayed out her lifetime of eighty-nine years with his Catholicized tribe.

New Englanders could read and did read. Books, especially one as dramatic as John Williams' story, were a good way to rouse and unify them. The Williams narrative went into sixteen editions. It was powerful propaganda for the colonists' determination to drive the French off the continent.

New England's few successes in Queen Anne's War, obtained without much cooperation from England, made the colonies self-confident. They were disgusted with the mother country's lack of support. They had no interest in the struggle for the balance of power in Europe. All they wanted was to oust the French from North America. Yet the war ended with France keeping Cape

Breton Island, which commanded the best entrance to the St. Lawrence River. There France built the mighty fortress of Louisbourg, a new threat to New England shipping.

The people of Massachusetts were no longer concerned only with freedom to worship as they chose. They began to demand other rights from their English government. They wanted freedom of speech and of the press, in order to criticize the government and express their hatred of tyranny. This would give them powerful propaganda. Propaganda would lead to action against English indifference and tyranny.

"The steel will always command the gold," Cotton Mather preached. "Men can have no right secured unto them if they do not make sure of might." The problem was to organize enough might to secure right. Money was one means.

The paper money grew in volume and shrank in purchasing power. Gold and silver were drained off to England, whose mer-

This engraving of Harvard in 1725 shows that New England had become wealthy enough to support riding horses, coaches, and footmen. Harvard Hall (at left) and Massachusetts Hall (at right) are still in use.

chants had to be paid in it. The merchants of Massachusetts, led by Elisha Cooke, saw that the best way to save the financial situation in the colony was to found a bank of credit.

Such an institution was hateful to the old-line Puritan ministers, for the Bible forbade taking interest on loans. But the merchants could talk about social measures and put them into action without going to the Bible for instruction or justification. Their bank would be incorporated on the security of land. The money it issued would save New England's trade from decay. The bank released its first fifty thousand pounds on November 5, 1715.

The merchants had defied the ministers, and won. Now the merchants could even sway the town meetings. New England was rich again, and everyone wanted a share in the prosperity.

When hostilities broke out again in Europe, New England leaped into the North American phase, known as King George's War. The money was at hand to make the New Englanders' dream of capturing Louisburg a reality.

The merchants of Maine, which was now under the jurisdiction of Massachusetts, descended on Governor Shirley in Boston, and urged him to send a force against that "Gibraltar of the New World." The Boston merchants joined them, and eventually persuaded the General Court to vote for the expedition. The command went to a Maine merchant, William Pepperrell.

Pepperrell, of Kittery, had made a fortune as his father's partner in West Indies trade. He owned huge tracts of Maine land. The Maine towns sent him as their representative to the General Court in Boston. There he married into the highly respected Puritan family of Judge Samuel Sewall, got a place on the governor's council, became its president and also chief justice of the superior court. He was known for his practical good sense, and he was successful, hence popular.

Governor Shirley knew the power of propaganda. Persuasive reports about the coming expedition went to other colonies. Connecticut responded with 500 men; they came in their own transports, led by Roger Wolcott, who was made second in command of the whole force. New Hampshire sent 450 men. Rhode Island sent an armed ship. New York, New Jersey, and Pennsylvania sent cannon

The Rosa Americana, a coin used in the colonies, with a portrait of King George I of England. King George's War was named for his son, George II.

and provisions. Maine and Massachusetts raised 3000 men. Governor Shirley got Commodore Peter Warren, who owned New York's Greenwich Village, to bring three 40-gun warships from his West Indies squadron. For once the colonies were truly united in a joint effort against a common enemy.

The huge fleet sailed from Nantasket on March 24, 1745, for a rendezvous at Canseau, Nova Scotia, which it recaptured from the French. It left there on April 29, and reached Louisbourg the next morning. For six weeks the American forces besieged the well-nigh impregnable fortress with bombardments, commando tactics, and fearfully hard work.

The Gloucester men had celebrated their departure at Peg Wesson's tavern. The more rum they consumed, the more they teased their hostess. Finally she peppered them with fire from her tart

William Pepperrell, his wife and children, with their pets and a table game. The family portrait is by John Singleton Copley.

New England tongue.

"Ah, Peg, you're a witch!" they taunted her. "When we get home we'll string you up like old Goody Nurse at Salem."

"Witch am I?" Peg Wesson screeched. "I'll witch you! You'll never take Louisbourg."

Fever and dysentery struck the men in their tents around the 30-foot-high walls of Louisbourg. Day after day an enormous rusty crow wheeled and cawed over their camp. They shot at it, but they could not bring it down.

Someone remembered Peg Wesson's threat. She was a witch indeed, and only a silver bullet could harm her.

They loaded a musket with a silver button from an officer's uniform. Their best marksman took careful aim. The crow let out a piercing shriek and flapped away.

That night, the men learned later, a doctor was called to the tavern in Gloucester. He cut a silver button from an officer's uniform out of Peg Wesson's leg.

The fortress of Louisbourg surrendered on June 17. New England surged with joy and pride. The colonies had mounted a major

Below: Landing of the New England forces at Louisbourg, 1745. Above: Figure of Britannia, with her spear and shield, from a flag carried by the New Englanders at Louisbourg.

military campaign with their own men and their own money, and won. And they had learned to work together.

Then the peace treaty of 1748 handed Louisbourg back to the French. The men who survived the terrible siege—hauling cannon, two hundred men to a gun, under fire, to set them against the walls—never forgot the insult from their ungrateful mother country. The peace lasted eight years.

Not all was peace, however, in the souls of New Englanders. Witchcraft was officially done with, but the sharp tongue of a vulgar tavernkeeper like Peg Wesson could uncover the fear of the Devil and his Hell which lurked in the minds of a people torn between their old faith and their new practicality.

Jonathan Edwards was a solitary child who talked of his love for God as if the deity were a pretty girl. He was the only boy of his parents' eleven children. He had a keen mind. He mastered Greek and Hebrew, Newton's new mathematics and Locke's new philosophy, and he experimented with prisms and the habits of spiders. He graduated from Yale in 1720 before he was seventeen.

Edwards went to his grandfather Stoddard's parish in Northampton, where the merchants of the Connecticut River—the "River Gods"—lived in splendor. The young minister preached so vividly about Hell that one of these rich, powerful men cut his own throat rather than go on living in dread of eternal torture.

Jonathan Edwards' congregation, especially the young, loved to weep with sorrow over their sins, and to moan that their minister pity them, and to swoon with terror at his pictures of God's wrath. They believed him when he predicted: "How dismal will it be when you are under those racking torments to know assuredly that you never, never shall be delivered from them . . . when you shall wish that you might be turned into a toad or a serpent, but shall have no hope of it . . . and when you shall have worn out the age of the sun, moon, and stars in your dolorous groans and lamentations . . . yet you shall have no hope, but shall know that you are not one whit nearer to the end of your torments."

Edwards did preach God's mercy as a kind of contrast to His anger, but he was not so apt at describing it.

Religion revived in Northampton, and the revival spread through all New England, so intellectually gifted was the Reverend Jonathan Edwards. Then George Whitefield came from England and preached the same dire message so dramatically that even Harvard undergraduates wept, and five persons were crushed to death in a crowd that came to hear him.

For five years this "Great Awakening" plunged New Englanders into an orgy of doubt and remorse and repentance. Then Edwards' flock rebelled because he accused the young people of reading indecent literature. It was no more than a handbook on childbirth, a subject that every child on the frontier knew about at first hand anyway. And Edwards' timing was poor; he fussed about his salary while his congregation fussed about his criticizing their children. They turned him out, and went back to the more immediate problems of making more money and fighting another war.

Jonathan Edwards went to minister to the frontiersmen and the Indians at Stockbridge, and after seven years in that outpost was called to be president of Princeton College. He had written many books during his exile at Stockbridge. One of these, *Freedom of the Will,* is among America's greatest philosophical works. He got to New Jersey at the height of a smallpox epidemic, and died on March 22, 1758, five weeks after reaching Princeton.

The Seven Years' War (in America, the French and Indian War) broke out in Europe in May, 1756. Massachusetts' Governor Shirley organized the New Hampshire woodsmen into Rangers, and made Robert Rogers their captain. They were to be scouts in the woods, the eyes and ears of the colonial forces. One of the lieutenants was John Stark, of Londonderry, New Hampshire.

Robert Rogers was as big as a moose and almost as ugly. He could lope through the woods like a lynx, and he knew all the tricks of the Indians. For his father had moved from Methuen in Massachusetts to the forest near Dunbarton, New Hampshire, where the boy grew up to be a broad-shouldered, slim-hipped giant.

Rogers' Rangers harassed the French and their Indian allies along Lake Champlain, the waterway from the St. Lawrence River

Jonathan Edwards. The painting is by Joseph Badger, one of Boston's most popular portrait painters.

into the interior of western New England. In one battle with the Indians, Rogers was shot in the wrist. A Ranger quickly cut off his pigtail and bound up the wound with it, and Rogers went on fighting.

Rogers and his men moved against strategic St. Francis (Odanak), fifty miles down the St. Lawrence from Montreal, from which gory raids into New England were being launched. They fell upon it on the night of October 2, 1759, after a riotous wedding celebration among its Christianized Indians, and shot or stabbed some two hundred of them as they were sleeping off the party. Then they set fire to every hut, looted the Catholic church, and headed south to Lake Memphremagog and the Connecticut River. On a fearful march back to the English forts, the Rangers lost forty-nine men, though only one had been killed at St. Francis.

Robert Rogers, 1776. In the background of the portrait are friendly Indians with their tomahawks.

But the colonial families on the frontier slept better now that St. Francis had been exterminated. Rogers had found six hundred settlers' scalps there.

Until then the war had gone badly for the English. Their commanders were weak, and they bungled and bickered. Then the ineffectual war minister in London was replaced with the brilliant young William Pitt. The tide of battle turned in America, and the war ended with the surrender of Canada to England in 1763. The menace of the Indians to the colonists vanished with that of their French allies.

Settlers from Connecticut streamed into the danger-free New Hampshire grants, which included the present state of Vermont. New York claimed the land under an English law, but New Hampshire's Governor Benning Wentworth kept selling "rights" in the region between Lake Champlain and the Connecticut River. The rival colonies decided to let the settlers fight it out among themselves.

Drawing believed to be a portrait of Ethan Allen

Ethan Allen came back home from the war to Cornwall, Connecticut, full of ambition to make a fortune in the lands he had seen while serving in the north. Six other Allen children worked on their father's pig farm; not much chance for a fortune there.

Ethan was a big man and a strong one and a mighty drinker and tavern brawler. Still he read a great deal and thought about the

Eleazar Wheelock, first president of Dartmouth College. Dartmouth was the fourth and last college founded in New England before the Revolution. The others were Harvard, Yale, and Brown.

books afterward, and he had wit and a gift for robust profanity, and he could talk anyone into anything.

Ethan talked his brothers Ira and Heman and Levi into moving up the Housatonic River to Salisbury, where the best iron in the colonies lay under the granite of Mt. Riga. He started an iron foundry there, while Heman and Levi set up a factory and made deerskin shirts and breeches. Ira, the youngest, worked for them and studied surveying. He was a quiet boy, but he had brains.

Ethan began speculating in New Hampshire grants. He went up into the Vermont woods and organized a posse of Green Mountain Boys to keep the New Yorkers off their land. When they caught one snooping, they stripped him and beat him with birch boughs until he fainted. The government of New York declared them outlaws.

Ira went up to survey the Allens' land. He was sick with measles, and then he got boils, and he came down with dysentery. But he talked Ethan and Heman into consolidating their grants on the Onion (Winooski) River before the New Yorkers might get them by right of previous surveying.

The Allens and their Green Mountain Boys scared the New Yorkers off, largely through Ira's demonstration of his skill at target-shooting with a pistol, and Ira surveyed the land for his brothers. Then they built a fort at the falls of the river. But, wrote Ira, "we never walked out without at least a case of pistols. In this situation we were a terror to the New York claimants."

Benning Wentworth's nephew John succeeded him as governor in 1766 when he was twenty-nine years old. He was a rich young man, for his father Mark was one of the twelve to whom the old Gorges-Mason land patents of the Laconia region had descended. Good-looking John had been to Harvard, and was socially ambitious and very popular.

The people of New Hampshire gave John Wentworth a booming welcome home from a trip to England, where he had worked hard for the colonies and got an honorary degree from Oxford. Then he set about reconciling the three separate interests in his colony of New Hampshire: the simple Connecticut farmers in the west; the settlers from Massachusetts in the Merrimack River valley; the old, rich, seafaring families of Portsmouth. His means was to connect them with roads. Once these had opened up the forest, new settlers flocked in. The region could be protected because the militia could move with ease and rapidity on Wentworth's highways from seacoast to Lake Champlain.

Up from Connecticut over these roads came missionary Eleazar Wheelock to start a school for Indians in newly settled Hanover. He was followed by his wife in a carriage, thirty students who walked, two Indians who refused to drive the cows, and a baggage wagon driven by his nephew and containing at least one barrel of New England rum.

The school, which became Dartmouth College, held its first commencement in 1771. Wheelock suffered trials that would have broken a less dedicated man. One of the most vexing was the charge that he had been inhospitable at the commencement exercises. "My wife has been ill," he apologized, "the cook was drunk, and besides, the college has only one tablecloth."

In Connecticut, a Collegiate School had finally been founded in Saybrook in 1701 and had moved to New Haven in 1716. In 1718 it was renamed Yale at the suggestion of Cotton Mather that this rechristening was the best way to thank its generous benefactor Elihu Yale.

Cotton Mather was invited to be Yale's first president, but he declined. He did not want to leave Boston, for he hoped to be president of Harvard. The election went to another, however, and Cotton Mather raged at "the slight and spite put upon him."

Mather would have had a terrible time at New Haven. He was not noted for his tact or diplomacy, and Yale's early problems needed both. In his place the founders chose the Reverend Abraham Pierson to head their institution for the instruction of youth "in the arts and sciences, who through the blessing of Almighty God may be fitted for public employment both in Church and Civil State."

The founders pretended that young Connecticut men who wished to be ministers needed a place of advanced education nearer home than Cambridge. But their real motive was to keep the congregational way free from the new philosophical ideas which had

James Bowdoin III about 1760, when boys (like their fathers) wore knee breeches. After the Revolution his father and he founded and endowed Bowdoin College in Brunswick. They were Boston merchants, and Maine was still part of Massachusetts.

Dartmouth College in 1803, as drawn by an 11-year-old member of the sophomore class.

been creeping into Harvard. Arguments over this and over the location of the new college almost strangled it at birth.

But by the time Dartmouth was founded, Yale was about to enter one of its greatest periods under such presidents as Ezra Stiles. and the first Timothy Dwight.

An informal ballgame at Yale, 1807.

In Providence, Rhode Island College—later Brown University —had been established in 1764. True to the spirit of tolerance in the colony, its charter stated that "all the members shall forever

enjoy full, free, absolute, and uninterrupted liberty of conscience." Such could not be said for Harvard or for Yale or for Dartmouth.

In spite of Rhode Island's tolerance, Newport was the slave market of New England. Its wealth came principally from the vicious circle of New England trade: lumber and commodities to the West Indies; molasses from those islands to New England, where it was turned into rum; rum to Africa to be bartered for slaves; slaves to the West Indies to work the plantations. Some slaves were brought to New England to be domestics in the merchants' mansions.

Newport's pleasant summer climate attracted visitors, especially from the southern colonies. It was already a summer resort in the eighteenth century, cosmopolitan, rich, beautiful. The aggressive Newport merchants, like Abraham Redwood, lived in patrician style with town houses near their wharves, and country seats like those of English squires. They made a point of broadening their town's outlook, and patronized arts and letters.

Portrait painters found plenty of patrons in colonial Newport. Gilbert Stuart, later one of America's greatest artists, was born in Narragansett across the bay, and learned to paint in Newport. The colony supported a fine silversmith. The British philosopher, Bishop George Berkeley, spent three years in Newport. His influence led to the formation of a philosophical club, which later became the Redwood Library. Peter Harrison, America's first architect, designed a beautiful classical building to house it.

New England's Gilbert Stuart was the most prominent American artist of his time.

Rhode Island tolerance attracted Jewish merchants as early as 1658, when Jews were not welcome elsewhere in New England. They engaged chiefly in the whale-oil trade and in candlemaking, Newport's chief industries. By 1763 there was a sizable congregation of Jews there. Peter Harrison built them the handsome Touro Synagogue, named for Isaac de Touro, a Portuguese Jew who found freedom from persecution in Rhode Island.

Newport was not alone in its luxury and refinement. Boston borrowed Peter Harrison to design King's Chapel, its first Anglican Church building. John Singleton Copley was making sophisticated portraits of the rich Boston merchants and lawyers and their wives, dressed in silks and satins, seated in graceful chairs at highly pol-

73

ished tables and admiring their gleaming silverware. Trade and its rewards had changed the old homespun cottons and linens into velvets and laces and ribbons from Europe, and severe provincial styles into the fashions of London and Paris.

Cramped medieval wooden buildings decayed and burned. Brick structures based on the generous baroque designs of European architects replaced them. Boston's Faneuil Hall and old State House and Old South Meetinghouse; Newport's Brick Market; New Haven's Connecticut Hall on the Yale Campus; and private houses like Governor Shirley's in Roxbury show the classicism— that is, the imitation of the standards of ancient Greece and Rome —which suited the ideas of the Age of Reason in Europe.

This new era in human thinking was a revolution against medieval superstition. It took reason instead of faith as the authority for human conduct. The basis of reason is realities—looking at things as they are. Reason is the enemy of superstition and can destroy superstition. Reason tries to find the true causes for things. Superstition either fails to find causes or accepts incorrect ones. Reason directs human beings to question whether a thing needs to be the way it is, not merely accept it.

The conditions of human life, therefore, do not have to stay the same. They can be changed for the better. Reason helps people make the most of themselves—that is, perfect or complete themselves—on earth. They do not have to wait for such happiness in some mysterious heaven which they can reach only through some mysterious means. The pursuit of happiness is the right of every human being. No other human being should be allowed to take that right away or keep anyone from using his reason or any other means of finding happiness for himself.

As these revolutionary ideas seeped into the New England mind, the pursuit of happiness by means of reason became part of the

Paul Revere at his workbench (1765) by John Singleton Copley. Copley usually painted fashionable New Englanders in their elegant clothes, as shown on page 65. Revere made beautiful silverware for the fashionable New Englanders.

New England Way. New England thinking, as usual, became New England action as soon as a leader appeared.

Samuel Adams studied the new ideas at Harvard. He got his master's degree for a thesis defending the right of a people to oppose their ruler if he keeps them from working for their common good in the way they have agreed with one another to do.

For the next twenty years Sam Adams talked politics along this line of reasoning. His platform was that the taxes England was imposing on her colonies were unjust. The colonies had not agreed to them. Furthermore, the tax money was paying the salaries of officials who were curtailing the right of the colonies to govern themselves. That right was what they had fought the wilderness to get.

The taxes were ruining the merchants. Because the city merchants were being ruined, so were the country farmers and the laborers. None of these classes had any legal power to protect themselves. Sam Adams said that they would have to rebel against a policy that was keeping them from working for their common good.

Samuel Adams (above) and John Hancock. Portraits of both Revolutionary leaders are by Copley, a Tory, who later moved to London.

Sam Adams got rich merchants like John Hancock, and brilliant lawyers like James Otis, to listen to his reasoning. He also got Boston's disgruntled workers on his side; he showed them that what was bad for their bosses was bad for them. He was a rousing speaker and he knew the power of propaganda and he was a good organizer—in short, a master politician. He finally got himself elected representative of Boston's town meeting in the General Court.

Now he could work at the machinery of New England self-government. He reasoned with the representatives of other town meetings throughout all the regions under Massachusetts jurisdiction. He circulated letters among the other colonies to keep them informed of what Massachusetts was doing. They were to keep in touch with one another and work together against any act of tyranny. For tyranny, Sam Adams shouted, was as sure to come as rain in New England, and it must be prepared against. Every New England farmer who had seen his crop of hay threatened by thunderheads piling up on the horizon knew what Sam Adams was talking about.

JOIN OR DIE

New England's colonies were not the only ones hit by the financial depression that followed the French and Indian War and by the heavy taxation England imposed in order partially to pay her war debt and the costs of administering the territories in America which England had won from France. Sam Adams saw that all the colonies should unite in their rebellion against their common oppressor. He set up a system of communication among them.

Sam Adams had already organized the Boston merchants and got them to sign an agreement not to import English goods on which England had placed a duty. England's trade would thus be damaged, just as the merchants' trade was being ruined by English duties and taxes. Through his communications with the other colonies, Adams got their merchants to do the same.

Next Sam Adams went to the taverns where Boston's dock workers would gather to talk about the depression. They could do nothing about the situation except grumble; they were not property owners and so could not vote.

Samuel Adams had real sympathy for the underprivileged. He had no money of his own, and he had no ability at getting money or handling it. He had been such a failure as a tax collector that he almost landed in jail; he just could not bear to squeeze taxes out of poor people like himself. So he got rich John Hancock to set up drinks for the workmen in their taverns, and then easily convinced them that in a new system they could vote and their vote would count as much as Mr. Hancock's. He organized them.

They called themselves the Sons of Liberty, but they were actually slaves to the firebrand oratory of Samuel Adams and the other merchant and lawyer intellectuals: James Otis, John Hancock, William Molineaux, Jonathan Mayhew, Josiah Quincy, Joseph Warren, and the radical journalists who wrote under the pen name of Joyce, Jr. When the speeches and the free drinks had roused these rough laborers sufficiently, they would roam the dark Boston

For a patriot newspaper, the Massachusetts Spy, *Paul Revere portrayed a divided American snake confronting a fierce British beast. He showed the New England colonies as a unit. Revere based this design on an earlier cartoon by Benjamin Franklin, the Pennsylvania patriot, who lived and worked in Boston until he was seventeen.*

streets, molesting non-sympathizers (Tories), breaking windows, burning boats, and hanging English tax commissioners and customs collectors in effigy from the Liberty Tree (a big elm at the corner of present Washington and Essex Streets). Many Tories moved away.

All through the long hot summer of 1765, Sam Adams and his liberal friends kept prophesying the tyranny to come. On the broiling hot night of August 26, the Sons of Liberty began to move. A mob of hoodlums closed in on the elegant house of Lieutenant Governor Thomas Hutchinson, ransacked it from top to bottom, and drove the Hutchinsons for refuge to Milton, fourteen miles from Boston.

Having, as it were, tasted blood, the Sons of Liberty thirsted for more, and kept up their mob activities. To keep order in Boston, England garrisoned two more regiments of red-coated soldiers there. The Boston ladies had a fine time with the officers, but the simpler people regarded the "lobster backs" as an unmitigated nuisance and an insult as well.

Sam Adams got his Sons of Liberty to pester the soldiers. There were squabbles and scuffles as the regulars retaliated against the rock-filled snowballs and sharp oyster shells thrown at them. All

To keep order in Boston, the British had to send additional troops in 1768. This engraving is by Paul Revere, one of the rebels who forced all the British troops to withdraw seven years later. The Old State House (also shown on page 90) may be seen at the far left.

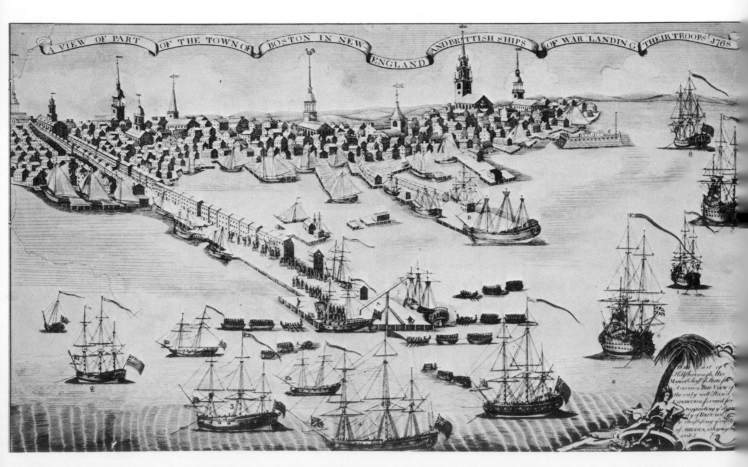

that was needed was for some rabble-rouser to touch off both sides. On March 5, 1770, some "tall man" did just that. The soldiers fired on the teasing mob which had whipped itself up into a state of panic. The British bullets killed five Bostonians in the street outside the State House (the corner of present State and Congress Streets). The fracas quickly was named the Boston Massacre.

John Adams was Sam's second cousin and, at the age of thirty-five, thirteen years younger. He was also calmer, cleverer, more patient, and more logical. When the "massacre" occurred, John Adams was a poor, hard-working lawyer, chiefly occupied in land cases. He was far from unsympathetic to his cousin's patriotism, but his integrity came first.

All other Boston lawyers refused to undertake the defense of the British Captain Preston and eight of his soldiers against the charge of murder. John Adams determined to keep justice an eternal part of the New England Way. He took the unpopular case, and got six of his clients acquitted on a plea of self-defense. His action won him the admiration of the patriots. John Adams began to rise as a power for freedom with reason, and also with order.

On the very day of the Boston Massacre, Parliament in faraway England abolished all the hated duties except on tea.

The trial of the British soldiers brought out how small a number of Bostonians had stirred up so much trouble. People grew tired of Sam Adams' dismal predictions of the tyranny to come, and they were sick of the ruffianly behavior of his Sons of Liberty. They did not mind the small tax on tea. Much of their tea was smuggled in from Holland anyway.

Then, to save the British East India Company from bankruptcy, England gave it a monopoly of the tea trade with America. No other merchants, including Boston ones, could deal in tea, and there were not even sales commissions for established American tea dealers.

This action alarmed the colonists all over again. Soon there might be a monopoly on other necessities as well. Sam Adams' party revived. He organized the first of many Committees of Correspondence (or Committees of Safety) which spread throughout the American colonies.

Engrav'd Printed & Sold by PAUL REVERE BOSTON

To arouse the American colonists, Paul Revere portrayed the Boston Massacre as if the British troops had deliberately fired on the Bostonians.

Adams called meetings of protest at Faneuil Hall and, when that proved too small for the masses who came, at Old South Meetinghouse. They were not regular town meetings, for non-voters were allowed to attend; they were called "Bodies."

One Body resolved to forbid the owner of Griffin's Wharf to unload an English tea ship, the *Dartmouth,* which had docked there on November 28, 1773.

Sam Adams sent the silversmith patriot Paul Revere on his first midnight ride. Revere was to warn the Committees of Safety in nearby seaports that other tea ships, after learning what had happened to the *Dartmouth,* might try to unload in their harbor.

Two more tea ships docked at Griffin's Wharf. The law was that they must be unloaded within twenty days. Governor Hutchinson refused to let them sail back to England with their cargo; that, too, would be illegal. Time was getting short.

Sam Adams called another Body on December 16. Seven thousand people came. There was wild oratory. Night fell. The younger men ran home from the Body, blackened their faces, wrapped blankets around themselves, and rushed back to Griffin's Wharf. They had been well organized beforehand, and given instructions on how to behave at a tea party.

Thousands watched as these "Indians" swarmed on to the ships and dumped the chests of tea into Boston Harbor.

Paul Revere carried the news of the Boston Tea Party to the patriots of New York and Philadelphia.

The British Prime Minister, Lord North, now made the great mistake of losing his temper. He closed the port of Boston to all commerce, quartered some four thousand troops on the citizens, made their General Thomas Gage governor, and ordered all serious lawbreakers to be tried in England, where witnesses could not give evidence for them.

Through the Committees of Safety Boston appealed for help to neighboring towns. They responded with overland shipments of supplies, for they saw that the situation affected them as much as it hurt Boston. It was time for them to take action. The town meetings elected delegates to a Provincial Congress which met illegally at Concord and made it impossible for Governor Gage's legal assembly to function; most of its members had gone to Concord.

By October, 1774, the Provincial Congress had set up the framework of a new government for Massachusetts, taken over tax moneys to buy ammunition, and called out the militia. It was rebellion, but it was also an orderly reaction to the crisis. The entire procedure was based on New England's ancient institutions of self-government—its reason and its rights.

For six months the towns drilled their "minutemen," the younger members of the militia, who were prepared to fight at a minute's notice. The patriots also stored military supplies in the churches. Governor Gage sent to England for reinforcements for his small army of occupation.

Parliament declared Massachusetts in a state of rebellion. The Secretary of War ordered Gage to seize the rebel leaders and end the uprising before it got bigger. Reluctantly—for he knew it meant war—Gage ordered his grenadiers and light infantry to capture the military stores which spies informed him the colonists

The Boston Tea Party attracted much attention in Europe. This picture appeared in Germany in 1784. A British version of the episode is shown in the background of the cartoon on page 85.

Statue of a minuteman standing at the head of Lexington Green.

had collected at Concord, and on the way take into custody Samuel Adams and John Hancock, who were at Lexington, six miles from Concord.

It was easy enough for the patriots in Boston to learn these plans. Paul Revere rode out to inform Adams and Hancock of them. They agreed that when it was clear on what day the British would come, and whether by the easy water route or by land, Revere would rouse the countryside.

On Tuesday, April 18, 1775, the news reached Paul Revere that the soldiers would move on the next day and by land. That night he set out on his famous ride to Lexington.

By the time the British light infantry got there, just after sunrise, Adams and Hancock were safe, and seventy-seven minutemen were armed and waiting for the redcoats on Lexington Green.

The six companies of British regulars formed a straight line about 150 feet from the roughly assembled minutemen. Major Pitcairn rode up to them.

"Disperse, ye rebels," he shouted. "Ye villains, disperse. Lay down your arms. Why don't ye lay down your arms?"

Veteran Captain John Parker addressed the armed farmers: "Don't fire unless fired on, but if they mean to have a war, let it begin here."

The two companies faced each other, every man's finger on the trigger, all growing tenser by the second.

Then a musket flashed, probably from a window or from behind a stone wall.

Immediately the British responded with scattered shots, and then with a volley. The minutemen answered. Then Captain Parker ordered them to withdraw. The British chased them until Major Pitcairn got his men back into line and marched them on to Concord. One was wounded, and so was Pitcairn's horse.

Ten of the minutemen were wounded, and eight were dead.

Riding to safety in a carriage, Samuel Adams heard the firing. "Oh, what a glorious morning this is!" he exclaimed.

John Hancock, his companion, thought he was referring to the weather. It had been an early spring, and the day was already warm. But Sam Adams was thinking of his country's freedom, little knowing that his part in securing it was almost over. He had got the machinery of independence ready; more cool-headed engineers than he were to run it.

The British entered Concord unopposed about eight in the morning of April 19. Colonel Francis Smith's grenadiers had by now joined Major Pitcairn's infantry. The soldiers got breakfast, which they paid for. They were dumping what flour and bullets they could find into the creek, when word came that the local

The battle of Lexington, as shown in an early lithograph

Colonel Smith and Major Pitcairn just before the battle at Concord Bridge. This detail is from a picture drawn by Ralph Earl, who was an eyewitness of the battle, and engraved by Amos Doolittle for propaganda purposes in 1775.

militia, which had gathered four hundred strong across the Concord River, was marching on the bridge at the north end of town. Colonel Smith led his men out to reinforce the small detachment he had sent to destroy the bridge. They fired and killed two minutemen.

The militia, under Colonel James Barrett, returned the fire, killed three redcoats, and wounded nine. Among these were several British officers.

The redcoats broke ranks and ran back to the center of town. The famous battle of Concord Bridge had lasted about five minutes around nine o'clock in the morning.

Paul Revere's alarm had set the villagers to ringing the church bells. As these were heard by one town after another, men left off building a barn or plowing a field or teaching school, grabbed up a musket, and headed for Concord.

By noon Colonel Smith recognized that he was about to be surrounded. He started his men back to Boston. As they marched past stone walls and barns and farmhouses, more and more fell, hit by the good marksmen—3600 of them from fifty towns—who were lying in wait. It was dark before the British got to their camp on Bunker Hill in Charlestown. By then, 274 were dead, wounded, or missing.

The rebels counted 93 casualties.

Three days later the Provincial Congress met at Watertown, seven miles west of Boston, and voted to raise 13,500 troops in Massachusetts. It gave the command to testy old Artemas Ward, who had been a general in the French and Indian War.

At ten o'clock of the "glorious morning" Israel Bissell had set out from Watertown with a letter containing the story of the fight at Lexington and instructions "to alarm the country quite to Connecticut." Bissell rode so hard that his horse dropped dead in Worcester that night. The next morning he got a fresh horse, and rode on.

In Brooklyn, Connecticut, Bissell found Colonel Israel Putnam plowing. "Old Put" had been one of Rogers' Rangers, had been captured by Indians and almost burned alive, and had been shipwrecked in a naval expedition against Havana. His strength and courage had made him a legend in the country. He heard Bissell's news and, without even waiting to unhitch his team, ran to collect his minutemen.

By Saturday afternoon, April 22, Bissell had spread the message of revolution as far west as Fairfield. On April 26, Governor Jonathan Trumbull called the Connecticut Assembly into special session to prepare for war. The Assembly ordered Israel Putnam to Massachusetts with 6000 Connecticut militiamen.

The news of Lexington and Concord reached York, Maine, on the evening of the fight. The Maine towns had dumped British tea, and their mobs had roughed up many a British tax collector. Colonel Samuel Thompson, of Brunswick, had captured British Captain Henry Mowatt for daring to seize the guns and the ammunition at Fort Pownall (now Fort Point, in Prospect, Maine) in March, 1775. One by one, the other towns of Maine learned

One unfortunate tax collector was tarred-and-feathered in Maine, and again in Boston. Although he was also forced to drink tea, he was not seriously harmed. As indicated by this British cartoon the Stamp Act, passed by Parliament to raise taxes, was particularly hated by the Americans.

that patriot blood had been spilled in Massachusetts, and sent their men to Cambridge, where the army was gathering.

New Hampshire sent 2000 men under Colonel John Stark. Rhode Island sent about 1000 under General Nathanael Greene.

The commanders of this New England army had got plenty of fighting experience in the French and Indian War, and so had some of their men. But they were poorly equipped, and they had no artillery, only their own muskets. And they were poorly organized, mostly ill trained, quarrelsome, and totally unused to military discipline.

About all they could do to advance the conflict was to encircle the British in Boston with siege works of earth and brush mats—a barbed arc that cut off all land approaches to the city and immobilized the British army. For six weeks the war was a stalemate.

When Ethan and Ira Allen heard of the shots at Lexington, they realized that unless Ticonderoga and Crown Point, two British forts on the New York shore of Lake George, were got into American hands, the British could isolate New England. Ethan sent Gersham Beach—Vermont's Paul Revere—on a sixty-mile ride to call the townsmen of Rutland, Pittsford, Brandon, Middlebury, and Whiting to a meeting in Castleton. Beach accomplished this extraordinary journey through the forest in twenty-four hours.

Ira Allen

Heman Allen was in Hartford when Silas Deane and some other patriots there learned of the army's lack of artillery. They decided not to wait for the legislature to convene. They sent Heman with a commission for his brother to take Ticonderoga. Then they raised three hundred pounds and got Captain Edward Mott to recruit some men and join Ethan Allen at Castleton.

Thirty-four-year-old Benedict Arnold was a prosperous New Haven druggist, bookseller, and merchant-trader. He had always been restless. Twice he had run away from his apprenticeship to a druggist in order to fight in the French and Indian War. He was strong and daring and mischievous.

As soon as he heard of Lexington fight, Arnold rounded up his militia company and marched to Cambridge. Quickly he saw the army's need for artillery, and proposed to capture the guns of Ticonderoga. The Provincial Congress made him a colonel, and authorized him to recruit a regiment and proceed to the fort. Arnold got a few men together, marched them to Castleton, and arrived on the very night that Ethan Allen and his eighty-three Green Mountain Boys were assembling at Hard's Cove to cross Lake George and take the fort.

Arnold insisted that he and he alone had the authority to command the expedition. Allen and Arnold argued until they realized that they would have to start out or lose their opportunity for a surprise attack. They compromised; Ethan Allen would allow Benedict Arnold to march beside him at the head of the company, providing Arnold gave no commands.

About three in the morning of May 10, 1775, two boats carried less than half the men across the lake. They climbed through the shambles of the southern entrance to the decaying fort. The British garrison of forty-five men was asleep—all but a sentry. His musket misfired. By the time he had given the alarm, Allen and his Green Mountain Boys were swarming through the fortress.

Allen burst into Commander Delaplace's room and demanded the surrender of Ticonderoga. Delaplace was trying to pull on his breeches. "B-by w-whose authority?" he stammered.

"In the name of the great Jehovah and the Continental Congress," Ethan Allen replied, though he had no authority from either.

The fortress was handed over to these rough Vermont yeomen without a drop of blood lost. Sixty good cannon fell into their hands, as well as other military stores, and ninety gallons of rum. The latter was quickly put to use "for the refreshment of the fatigued soldiery," Ethan Allen wrote.

The next day Seth Warner, of Bennington, captured Crown Point.

In early June, 1100 reinforcements of General Gage's troops had arrived in Boston. And three younger generals: William Howe, John ("Gentleman Johnny") Burgoyne, and Henry Clinton. They planned to break out of the besieged city.

American spies reported this intention to the Provincial Congress in Watertown. The council of war decided to fortify Bunker Hill in Charlestown, from which they could fire on the town of

Roger Sherman of Connecticut was a delegate to the Continental Congress and helped to draft the Declaration of Independence. The portrait is by Ralph Earl.

Boston. But Colonel William Prescott decided on Breed's Hill instead because it was nearer Boston. On the night of June 16, 1775, his 1200 men dug a redoubt on its top.

The afternoon of June 17 was unbearably hot, but the heavily equipped redcoats began moving up the steep hill as if on parade, firing from time to time. The bullets went over the heads of the Americans.

Prescott knew how little ammunition he had. He told his men: "Don't fire until you can see the whites of their eyes."

When the British were close enough to charge the redoubt, the fence on the earthworks flamed. The deadly aim of men who had hunted since they were old enough to shoot mowed down the advancing scarlet line. It broke, re-formed, marched up the hill again, retreated once more. By the time the third advance of the British had reached the redoubt, the Americans were out of ammunition.

They fought fiercely with their musket butts and with stones, but they had to retreat. After a brief stand on Bunker Hill, they withdrew in order to Cambridge.

The Battle of Bunker Hill, as it was later named rather incorrectly, cost the British so many casualties that it was a moral victory for the Americans. They made the most of it in propaganda, demonstrating that the ragged American army could stand against a British force of greater numbers, greater training, and superior equipment.

The Continental Congress, consisting of delegates from all the colonies, had met in Philadelphia on the same day that Ticonderoga fell. Plump John Adams kept insisting they should send no more petitions to King George III of England. Revolution was a present fact, not a possibility that might be avoided. He persuaded the Congress to adopt the tatterdemalion army in Cambridge. The New England rebellion became the American Revolution.

A commander in chief was needed to replace ailing old Artemas Ward. John Adams put all his considerable influence behind the tall, silent delegate from Virginia, Colonel George Washington. A Southerner, Adams reasoned, would bring Southern men into the army. It would be a truly American army, not a provincial one.

On July 3, 1775, Washington arrived in Cambridge to take

The Battle of Bunker Hill. This drawing was made in 1786 by a German artist, who probably talked to eyewitnesses.

command. All the rest of the summer and into the fall, Washington drilled his men, pleaded with them to continue their enlistment, struggled to get them food and firewood and shelter. His wife Martha joined him; her charm bolstered sagging morale. There was little fighting, only an occasional bombardment.

Washington's objective was to get the British out of Boston, but he did not have artillery enough to dislodge them. He did have, however, 25-year-old Henry Knox.

Knox kept a bookstore in Boston's Cornhill and stocked it with military treatises for his British customers and studied them himself. He was only a civilian volunteer in Washington's army, but he knew more about military tactics than most professionals. He was plump; the punning Tory Mather Byles said of him: "I never saw an ox fatter," a joke that irritated Henry. When Washington first came to Cambridge, Henry Knox showed him around. Impressed, Washington made him colonel of artillery.

Henry Knox, a portrait by Gilbert Stuart

Knox remembered the cannon, the mortars, and the howitzers perching unused on the ramparts of Ticonderoga. He proposed to get them to Cambridge—an almost impossible undertaking, especially in winter. He convinced Washington that he could do it.

Along the way to Lake George, Knox hired strong frontiersmen, only too willing to get into the faraway action somehow. They tugged Ticonderoga's cannon down the slopes of the fort, rowed them down the lake and the Hudson and Mohawk Rivers on barges, loaded them on sleds, hitched the sleds to eighty-one yoke of oxen, dragged them over the Berkshire Hills and across Massachusetts to the lines Washington had drawn on Dorchester Heights commanding Boston. The effort took fifty days of exhausting toil in freezing weather, but only two small cannon were lost.

In early March, General Howe, who had replaced Gage, saw the mouths of Ticonderoga's cannon and mortars pointing down at his own feeble fortifications. He arranged for safe evacuation of his forces in exchange for his promise not to burn Boston. On March 17, 1776, the last British troops departed. Massachusetts was free.

From then on, New England was to be only a minor theater during the War of American Independence.

An American Revolutionary soldier, as engraved by Paul Revere for paper money issued by Massachusetts in 1775.

5·IMPROVING NEW ENGLAND

State Street (site of the Boston Massacre) and the Old State House after the Revolution. The Declaration of Independence had been read aloud from the State House balcony. The building is still in use and open to the public.

It was more than eight years before the bells in the steeples pealed again in New England as they had rung on the morning of Lexington and Concord. The war was formally over. John Adams and his fellow commissioners had negotiated a peace treaty in Paris that secured the new American nation's independence.

John Adams had labored for three years in the Continental Congress. He defended the Declaration of Independence, which he helped compose. He served on innumerable committees including the important Board of War. He went to Paris with his 11-year-old son John Quincy to make an alliance with France which helped the Americans win the war. He constructed a constitution for the

Commonwealth of Massachusetts to replace the hated old charter of 1691; later much of it was copied in the Constitution of the United States. He was ambassador to Holland. He was now having a few months of leisure at home in Quincy before leaving for London as American ambassador to the Court of St. James's.

His cousin Sam Adams represented Massachusetts in the Continental Congress, served in the senate of Massachusetts, was elected its lieutenant governor, and eventually its governor.

John Hancock was chosen president of the Continental Congress, scrawled his conceited signature ahead of all the other signers of the Declaration of Independence, and returned to Massachusetts to be its first independent governor—for eleven years.

Ethan Allen was captured by the British and taken in chains to London, where he was exhibited like a freak in a sideshow. Home again, he wrote a sturdy book on atheism. Pious President Timothy Dwight of Yale wrote in his diary on February 12, 1789: "This day Ethan Allen died and went to Hell."

Benedict Arnold drove the British out of his native Connecticut and led the American troops which broke the British lines at the Battle of Saratoga. Then, vexed at insults to his vanity, he sold himself to the British and joined the list of the world's most notorious traitors.

Rubbing from the gravestone of a patriot killed at the battle of Bennington. As a symbol of the soul's victory over death, the stonecutter showed a skull wearing a crown.

John Stark, the old Rogers' Ranger, got over his peevishness at not being promoted in the army. He saw the British-hired Hessians marching on Bennington. "There are the redcoats," he said, "and they are ours, or this night Molly Stark sleeps a widow." Then he led his Vermont militia to an important victory on August 16, 1777.

Paul Revere commanded an artillery train in the campaign to get the British out of Newport, Rhode Island. Then he led some 1800 raw militiamen, many of whom were only sixteen years old, on a poorly planned expedition to recapture Castine, Maine. He got them home again, unsuccessful but more or less safe. He settled down in Boston to manufacture clear-toned church bells and copper sheathing.

Fat Henry Knox became George Washington's trusted friend, and ably directed the artillery all through the Revolution, and was

John Adams of Quincy (above) was the second President of the United States.

His son, John Quincy Adams (shown below at the age of 28 in a portrait by Copley), was the sixth President of the United States.

rewarded with the post of Secretary of War. Later he bought up all the Maine land in the patent which belonged to his wife's family, got immigrants to settle on it, bought more, went into farming and brickmaking and shipbuilding, built himself a magnificent mansion at Thomaston in which a hundred guests could sleep at a time, and died in debt but owning two million acres of Maine land.

Not many of the veterans fared anywhere near so well after the war as Major General Henry Knox. Most of them came back from the campaigns to face a cruel financial depression all over New England. Farm prices plummeted. Speculating merchants bought up imported goods that had been lacking for eight years, and held them until prices skyrocketed. The currency was wildly inflated. Farmers, small tradesmen, the veterans themselves could not pay their bills or the high taxes. Creditors foreclosed mortgages.

Veterans in Massachusetts revived the old Committees of Safety. They could get no relief from the legislature, which was filled with profiteers interested in protecting their speculations, not in the welfare of the community as the colonial aristocrats had been.

Daniel Shays had fought at Lexington and Bunker Hill and Ticonderoga and Saratoga, and had been given a sword for his bravery. Now Captain Shays had to sell it for cash to save his home. Ruined farmers and laborers and mechanics formed regiments to march on the courts that were sentencing them to debtors' jail. They got angry Daniel Shays to lead an attack on the arsenal at Springfield to seize arms against any attempt to suppress them. They thought the defenders of the arsenal would join them, but instead these killed three of Shays' rebels.

In Boston, General Benjamin Lincoln had to go to the merchants for money for an expedition against Shays and his army, so empty was the Massachusetts treasury. The impoverished yeomen clashed with the troops of the rich seacoast merchants in Berkshire towns and in the Connecticut valley until Lincoln routed them at Petersham on February 4, 1787.

The issues that led to Shays' Rebellion did not exist in Massachusetts alone; all New England was more or less in the same crisis. Benjamin Lincoln's sordid little triumph in the snow meant

the end of the small farmer, and of agriculture as a major part of New England's economy. The property owners, stronger in the legislature, had won more than a skirmish. The landless saw themselves as a class forever defeated. Veterans who, in their campaigns, had seen the rich, free soil to the west sighed at the contrast with their mortgaged stony acres.

Farmers began to move out of New England and to build new lives and new communities in Ohio and Illinois and Indiana territory. The New England Way trekked across the Appalachians with them, for they could not forget the heartbreaking beauty of the glens of Connecticut and the strength of the Massachusetts hills and the calm of the ponds of Vermont and New Hampshire and Maine. Soon white-steepled meetinghouses broke the straight horizons of the prairies and comforted the pioneers, homesick and sad as they thought of their former fields reverting to paintbrush and goldenrod and their old barns crumbling.

Henry Knox's house in Thomaston, Maine

*Farms began to dot
the wilderness as Americans
moved west from
the Atlantic seaboard.*

New England turned again to the sea, and snatched prosperity
out of its waters. The British West Indies were closed to American
trade. But as shipbuilding revived after the war, the merchants
smuggled New England lumber and codfish and whale oil into
the Caribbean islands through ports held by Denmark and Holland. Americans could trade openly with French and Spanish
possessions. The overseas market revived for the summer produce
of the farmers and the woodenware they made in the winter. Some
of Shays' former rebels stayed put.

The Caribbean was far too small a sales area for the jack-of-all-
trades New Englanders, all the more ambitious and enterprising
now that they had their own free nation. They were free to move
in on the Far Eastern trade—silks and tea, spices and India cotton.
England's East India Company no longer could exclude them from
these fabulous riches.

John Ledyard's guardians sent him from Groton, Connecticut, all
the way to Dartmouth College so that he could learn to be a missionary to the Indians. John scandalized that institution, went to

live with the Indians, and finally paddled away from school in a handmade canoe down the Connecticut River. He joined the British marines and sailed with Captain Cook to the Pacific. Cook stopped at Vancouver and the Aleutians, and Yankee John Ledyard saw at once the fantastic possibilities of a fur trade with the Indians there. They were not much different from the ones he had lived with in New Hampshire, and they got on fine together. Ledyard met Thomas Jefferson in Paris and told him that furs which cost sixpence in Vancouver sold for one hundred dollars in China. Jefferson reported Ledyard's story to America, and Captain Robert Gray, from Tiverton, Rhode Island, thought about it and acted.

Gray convinced a group of Boston merchants that furs from the Pacific Northwest would be as good tender in China as silver money, which nobody in Massachusetts had anyway. They fitted out two ships and sent them around Cape Horn to Vancouver, where they spent a winter loading their holds with sea-otter skins. One ship remained there, but Robert Gray took the 212-ton *Columbia* across the ocean to Canton, swapped the furs for tea, and sailed her around Africa back to Boston. He had been gone three years.

The *Columbia* gave her home port, on that August 9, 1790, a salute of thirteen guns, and then another—in honor of the states of the nation. Bostonians rushed to the waterfront to cheer the first American ship to girdle the globe.

Other Yankee ships had visited Canton and brought back silks and teas and porcelains, notably those of Salem's Elias Hasket Derby—"King" Derby, they called him as his fleet and his fortune increased. But these ships had carried miscellaneous goods to trade, and their cargoes took a year to assemble and were expensive to boot. The *Columbia* had found the easy key to the empire New England would build on the China trade.

Masts and spars were magic wands that changed the postwar depression into undreamed-of prosperity. The treasures of the East flowed into the warehouses of Salem and Boston. Harborsides were jammed with shipyards, shipping offices, ropewalks, cooper shops, chandleries. All day they rang with the din of adzes and caulking

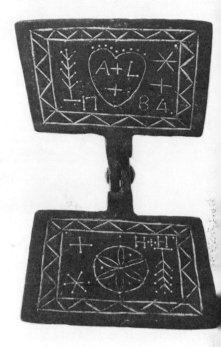

A New England wafer iron. The iron is heated in an open fireplace and removed while still hot. At a work table the batter is poured in and the wafer iron closed during baking.

A New England foot warmer, about 1790. It was filled with hot coals at home or a tavern, and carried to church for the lengthy service.

95

Shipbuilding in East Boston in the mid-nineteenth century. In the background the artist sketched Charles Bulfinch's "new" State House (completed in 1798) and the Bunker Hill Monument (1825).

irons, and ship after ship slid down the ways to fetch home the wealth of the Indies. Even in little Duxbury, twenty-eight ships would be under construction at one time; its Ezra Weston built a fleet and a shipping empire that earned him the name of "King Caesar." A hundred ships a year cleared the port of New Haven, bound for Canton, the only port of China open to Americans.

Trade with the West Indies and the Mediterranean countries also brought New England enormous profits. Ship captains bound for British ports abroad were willing to risk capture by French vessels, due to the war that revolution in France had brought about between that country and England—and almost with America too. One Maine captain joined a plot to rescue the French Queen Marie Antoinette from the French Terror, and he even got her household belongings onto his ship. But the plot failed, and the queen was rushed to the guillotine.

Barbary pirates from the states of Tunis, Algiers, Tripoli, and Morocco captured American ships trading in the Mediterranean and kept their men in slavery until ransomed. The United States paid some of this tribute, then refused to continue. Robbed of that revenue, the Pasha of Tripoli declared war in 1801.

96

Three years later Commodore Edward Preble, of Portland, Maine, sailed the frigate *Constitution* into Tripoli harbor and bombarded the town while his marines threatened it on land. The frightened pasha came to terms.

The *Constitution* had been designed by Joshua Humphreys of Philadelphia, and built at Edmund Hartt's shipyard where the Charlestown Navy Yard now is. Paul Revere had supplied her copper bolts, spikes, and staples, and had cast her bell. Her sails were made in Boston's old colonial grain storehouse—the only building large enough—which stood beside the ancient burying ground still called the Granary. The *Constitution* took to the waves on October 21, 1797, as all Boston cheered her. She was Boston's own ship, and Boston rewarded Edmund Hartt's "ability, zeal and fidelity in the completion of that ornament of the American Navy" with a silver tea set made by Paul Revere.

When the *Constitution* was overhauled in 1803, just before Preble took her to Tripoli, Paul Revere sheathed her hull in the copper sheets he had begun to make, an industry that became one of New England's outstanding ones. On August 19, 1812, under Captain Isaac Hull of Connecticut, the *Constitution* defeated the British *Guerrière* in the United States of America's first naval victory. It won her the nickname "Old Ironsides" because her hull was so little damaged by shot. Later that year she defeated the British *Java*.

From a Paul Revere advertisement for bells, brass cannon, and copper sheathing. Many bells made by Revere still ring in New England church steeples.

The bombardment of Tripoli by the Constitution. *The famous frigate, affectionately known as "Old Ironsides," may be visited today in the Charlestown Naval Shipyard.*

Nathaniel Bowditch, portrait by Gilbert Stuart

After the Revolution the eagle was a popular American symbol. This tavern sign shows a heart-shaped eagle holding an olive branch and an anchor.

The major part of the wealth brought home from abroad went to the merchants who owned the ships—the Sturgises, Derbys, Crowninshields, Perkinses, Westons—but officers were given room in the holds for their personal cargo. Soon they were shipowners too. Even the seamen prospered; wages at sea were better than on land, and they could usually work in a little trading. Every boy with gumption longed to sail to the East, and many who signed on at sixteen were captains at twenty and retired to enjoy their luxury at thirty.

Nathaniel Bowditch, the son of a Salem shipmaster whom the blockade of the Revolution had ruined, went to sea as a captain's clerk. He had a passion for mathematics. All through the long voyage to Manila he made celestial observations and taught some of the crew to get longitude without a chronometer, too expensive an instrument for a merchant ship. He found eight thousand errors in the standard book on navigation, which meant trouble for any ship that sailed by its inaccurate data. In 1801 he published his own version as *The New American Practical Navigator,* and demonstrated its efficiency by bringing his ship into Salem harbor through a Christmas Eve blizzard in which he could not pick up a single landmark. Guiding ships by primitive dead reckoning changed to expert navigation, which put American vessels far ahead of their competitors. Bowditch's book, regularly revised, is still a standard work of navigation.

Fortunes from shipping changed the appearance of New England's towns. (Towns they still were called; Boston did not become a city, for example, until May 1, 1822.) Shipowners and ship captains were at the top of society. Though few if any of them had much formal education or tradition of luxury, they wished to live in style. In Salem they commissioned Samuel McIntire to build their houses, and in Boston, Charles Bulfinch.

McIntire's father had taught him how to build a house. In his early twenties Samuel designed and constructed a mansion for Salem merchant Jerathmeel Peirce, still one of America's finest houses. McIntire set the style of the Federal Period—so called from the name of the political party which then represented the interests of the rich merchants.

Square, three-storied, hip-roofed, McIntire's brick houses have white wooden trim, pillared doorways, cupolas from which their ship-merchant owners could scan the horizon for homecoming sails. On the interiors McIntire lavished his skill as a woodcarver. His paneled rooms focus on a fireplace with a graceful carved mantel; their walls are topped with classical moldings.

On the rear of the house, a Palladian window—that is, one adapted from the three passages of a Roman triumphal arch—looks out over a formal garden toward stables and barns designed to blend with the house itself. Tall fountain elms shade the whole. Sometimes a white wooden fence with posts topped by classic urns encloses the grounds.

Salem's Essex Street, Washington Square, and Chestnut Street, to which the rich merchants retreated from the noisy waterfront, are almost exclusively the work of Samuel McIntire. They are

Above: A Salem house designed by Samuel McIntire. Below: Shield from gate of Salem Common, also made by McIntire, a skilled woodcarver.

99

among the world's most harmonious residential sections.

Charles Bulfinch was born in his aristocratic family's house in Boston's Bowdoin Square. He went to Harvard and he went to Europe, and he came home eager to make his beloved Boston as beautiful as the planned cities he had seen abroad.

Bulfinch learned a great deal from McIntire; both had learned from the Adam brothers of England. Bulfinch, however, was designing for Bostonians, who were more sophisticated and formal than the merchants of Salem. And so Bulfinch added bow fronts to break the outer stolidity of his square houses and permit oval rooms within. Stairways are free, curving as they rise, with delicate stair rails, banisters, and newel posts. They seem to float upward from spacious entrance hall to wide corridors above.

Bulfinch's state capitol in Boston set the style for other capitals from Augusta, Maine, to Washington, D.C. Other public buildings, like Harvard's University Hall, Bulfinch built of native granite which suits the slim but solid lines of his design. He remodeled

John Trumbull's portrait of his parents. His father, Jonathan Trumbull, was governor of Connecticut during the Revolutionary period—the only colonial governor who actively supported the Revolution.

old buildings like Boston's Christ Church ("Old North") and Faneuil Hall, keeping the best of their old elements while making their proportions more generous. He laid out crescents and colonnades to enhance the charm of his city. For a hundred years no other American architect surpassed him.

Asher Benjamin followed in Bulfinch's style, and built Boston's West Church, the Charles Street Meetinghouse, and the twin houses of 54-55 Beacon Street. Benjamin's work is clumsier than Bulfinch's, but undeniably elegant. He carried the style to Connecticut and Vermont and New Hampshire.

Painter Gilbert Stuart came back to New England from a successful career in London and Dublin, bringing with him his own version of the aristocratic British portrait style of Sir Joshua Reynolds and Thomas Gainsborough. Almost every Bostonian who could afford Stuart's prices sat to him. Stuart's sophisticated work —vivacious, subtle, with striking characterization, fine color, and brilliant brushwork—made him not only the greatest American painter of his day but influential for fifty years after his death in 1828.

In Connecticut, John Trumbull learned Stuart's style, and extended it to historical painting.

Literature began to flourish too, now that there was wealth to patronize it, peace in which it could be practiced, and a new nation with glorious prospects to celebrate. New Englanders had always written and written well, but their works conformed too much to the Puritan doctrine to rate as truly creative products of an independent mind. Even so, William Bradford's *Of Plymouth Plantation,* Cotton Mather's *Magnalia,* and Jonathan Edwards' *Freedom of the Will* have proved to be masterpieces.

Now, in Hartford, Connecticut, sprang up a group known as the Hartford Wits: John Trumbull, Timothy Dwight, Joel Barlow, Lemuel Hopkins, and a few others who glorified American subjects and American scenes and lusty American humor and the American dream of a golden age. And Noah Webster, a Yale graduate from West Hartford, was beginning his everlasting *An American Dictionary of the English Language* (published 1806-1828).

Noah Webster, a descendant of William Bradford, compiled two all-time best sellers—his spelling book and his dictionary.

An "American Sailor Boy," seized from an American merchant vessel to serve in the British navy. The drawing illustrated a poem published to arouse American indignation against the British practice of "impressment."

Hartford was now the intellectual capital of New England. Ideas were developing there that almost made New England a separate country. The independence of mind and action which had built a civilization in the wilderness kept New Englanders wary of joining their interests with those of regions different in climate, soil, economy, religion, and general point of view.

One by one the old colonies, now states, had agreed to accept the Constitution which united them politically. Rhode Island had held out to the very end. Only when told that it would have to sign up or be a separate nation of one thousand square miles of land area did it become the last of the thirteen colonies to join the union. Even so, Rhode Island kept her old seventeenth-century charter until 1842.

Vermont had actually been an independent republic from January 15, 1777, to March 4, 1791. Quarrels with New Hampshire and New York over what land was whose caused the Vermonters to rebel and practically drop out of the Revolutionary War. Ira Allen, modestly keeping in the background, wrote a constitution that other men argued over until, because of a thunderstorm that prolonged their meeting, they finally adopted it.

Ira intrigued and plotted to keep "New Connecticut," as the area was first called, free and in control of its lands, and he got it accepted into the union as the fourteenth state, Vermont, on its own terms. One-eyed, uneducated, homey Thomas Chittenden, who had come from Salisbury, Connecticut, with the Allens, was Vermont's governor for eighteen years. Vermonters felt that this huge fellow must be right even when he couldn't tell why he held certain opinions. He was a poor speaker anyway.

Even landlocked Vermont joined the rest of New England to assert the independence of the region when policies of the federal government threatened the prosperity that came from the sea.

Republican Thomas Jefferson, of Virginia, had succeeded New England's own Federalist John Adams as President. Jefferson's democratic ideas differed from those of the New England merchants, who were staunch and very vocal Federalists.

New England Federalists believed a central government's business was to protect property, especially commercial and shipping property like their own. They wanted a government run by rich, educated men. They had a low opinion of the administrative abilities of southern farmers who picked cotton instead of hoisting sails. Jefferson's policies they saw sacrificing New England's maritime commerce to the agriculture of the southern states.

Then instead of going to war with England over violations of neutral shipping, Jefferson forbade American ships to sail for foreign ports. He enforced this embargo with federal troops. New England's exports dropped. Even the China trade was affected, though it was hardly a part of the dispute with England. New England's shipbuilding fell off by sixty percent. Unemployment grew. Merchants went bankrupt. Mobs attacked revenue officers.

Hartford's Federalist thinking turned into action. Connecticut's Governor Trumbull refused to order the state militia to suppress riots. Rhode Island declared the embargo an act of tyranny. Massachusetts towns revived the old Committees of Safety. Vermonters took to smuggling goods into Canada. Radicals talked of getting New England out of the Union.

A party in Boston about 1820. The artist, Henry Sargent, showed the Federal-style interior of his house, as well as the new high-waisted gowns of the ladies.

Jefferson repealed the embargo, and the crisis seemed over. Then the new president, James Madison, also a southern Republican, in 1812 declared war on England—largely to protect the western territories from Indian raids supposedly instigated by English Canada.

New England had no interest whatever in this motive. Massachusetts, Connecticut, Vermont, and Rhode Island refused to lend their militia to "Mr. Madison's War," which was seriously damaging their shipping. New England would not grant any substantial war loans, although it was really the treasury of the nation. New England ships, before the British blockaded the ports, traded more or less openly with the enemy. Newspapers debated the question of secession.

In 1814 Connecticut's Assembly declared the Federal draft law unconstitutional, and also voted to join a convention to protest the poorly managed war. This convention had been called by a group of Boston merchants, led by George Cabot, who was elected its presiding officer. Theodore Dwight of Connecticut was named secretary. It met in Hartford on December 15, 1814, and kept its sessions secret.

The rich among the twenty-six delegates wanted to pull New England out of the Union, but the moderates restrained them. The convention merely passed resolutions for revisions of the Constitution that would give more protection to their own states' interests.

The sudden end of the war made the decisions of the Hartford Convention not only useless but ridiculous. Peace, and Andrew Jackson's victory at New Orleans, brought such joy that thoughts of secession were forgotten. The leaders of the Hartford Convention were ruined for future public life; the less propertied people regarded them as traitors. Federalism and New England's stubborn insistence on independence as a political unit lay like toppled statues.

New England actually suffered very little in this War of 1812. The British bombarded Stonington, Connecticut, but were prevented from landing. On the Maine coast, however, they captured Eastport and Robbinston, which gave them control of the Penobscot, and later Hampden and Bangor. The Maine militia surrendered. England claimed all the land between Penobscot and Pas-

Paul Revere's silverware changed with shifts in taste. The sturdy design of his tankard (above) gave way to the more delicate lines of his Federal-style teapot (below).

samaquoddy Bays as a province of Canada, and made their General Gosselin governor of it.

Although the British had successfully blockaded New England harbors by 1814, even bottling up the *Constitution* in Marblehead, New Englanders made plenty of money in privateering and smuggling. The dangers to legal shipping, however, fostered the beginning of industry.

England was too occupied with Napoleon in Europe—the War of 1812 with America was to England a minor item in that struggle—to compete with the New England mills. Industrial enterprises thrived. Roads were built in the interior of New England, and over them ox teams hauled manufactured goods toward southern markets previously reached by water.

By 1818 there were sixty-seven cotton mills in Connecticut alone, most of them close to Rhode Island, the only state in the region which exceeded Connecticut in the percentage of its people engaged in manufacturing. The demand for cloth was high, and the price of raw cotton was low, thanks to Eli Whitney's invention of the cotton gin.

Eli Whitney had a sharp mind and nimble fingers. The Whitney farm in Westboro, Massachusetts, did not produce enough cash to send young Eli to Harvard; so he set up a workshop in the barn and turned out handy things like nails that people could not buy easily during the Revolution. (People would give "nailing parties" at which guests pulled nails out of old boards and pounded them straight for a second use.)

Eli worked his way through Yale and got a tutoring job in Savannah, Georgia, and fell in love. To get enough money to marry, he invented an engine ("gin") to get the green seeds out of the short-staple cotton that grew all around. It could be run by hand or horsepower or waterpower, and it saved endless hours of hard work. He got a partner and built gins all over the cotton country and revolutionized cotton production.

Advertisement for regular stagecoach service between Boston and Providence. Many coaches of the time were made in Concord, New Hampshire.

105

Eli Whitney went back north to New Haven, and thought up a new way of making guns. Instead of one skilled craftsman making all the parts of a gun and putting them together, each of several unskilled men would make one part apiece with a power tool by a pattern that kept the parts alike. Then these separate parts could be put together into a finished gun by any number of men who had no other training. Once Whitney got these skill-saving techniques into operation in 1809, nine years after he had sold the idea to the government, he revolutionized New England industry.

The Whitney or "uniformity" system soon was applied to any number of different manufactures, saving time and money. It meant that only machines—not men—had to be limited to one process. It meant that a free mind, open to new kinds of pattern making, was more valuable than trained hands. Gone was the sharp distinction between skilled and unskilled labor, and with it the fear of unemployment which enslaves workers. The new system also meant that any man with a flexible mind could move from one degree of wealth to a higher one as easily as he could shift from one factory to another. The only things in American society that henceforth would stay rigid were the machines.

Above: Eli Whitney. The portrait is by Samuel F. B. Morse, another talented New Englander, who later invented the telegraph. Below: David Humphreys in his Revolutionary War uniform.

David Humphreys graduated from Yale and taught school until he joined Israel Putnam's militia. He acted as aide-de-camp to General George Washington and went to Paris as secretary to the peace commissioners after the Revolution. Then he came home to Derby, Connecticut, and collaborated with the Hartford Wits on a poem (*The Anarchiad*) which made fun of the political confusion, and became President Washington's private secretary, and was minister to Portugal and Spain.

Humphreys came back from Spain with one hundred merino sheep. When Jefferson's embargo cut off the wool supply from abroad, everyone wanted a pair of Humphreys' sheep to breed. Sheep raising became a mania in Connecticut, and Humphreys built a woolen mill at Derby and made a fortune. By 1818 there were sixty other woolen mills going full time in Connecticut, and two hundred fulling mills for thickening woolen cloth.

Vermont, whose towns had copied those of its mother state, Connecticut, now copied its wool mania. Humphreys' successor

in Spain, William Jarvis, shipped four thousand sheep to his home in Wethersfield in 1810. He sold many of them to Vermont farmers, for sheep fare better than crops on their rocky acres. A dark Spanish shepherd drove them up from Connecticut, singing strange songs with unintelligible words as he walked behind them, looking to neither right nor left. By 1840, there were over two million sheep in Vermont, and their fleeces brought the first prosperity to that struggling state. Many a Vermonter could afford a tall Greek-revival house in the style of that time, with a pillared porch like a Greek temple's, thanks to his flock of merinos.

All through New England, tanneries and flaxseed-oil mills, distilleries and iron foundries, arms factories and clothing manufactories (fifty-six hat shops in Danbury), clock and pottery works

Machine shops of the Chisel and Steel Square Works, Shaftsbury, Vermont, 1857. The manufacture of tools and machinery is still important in the state.

107

Above: Elias Howe, a portrait made by a new kind of artist, the photographer. Below: John Quincy Adams, whose oil portrait by Copley appears on page 92, lived long enough to sit for his photograph at the age of 79.

and paper mills hummed and belched smoke into the pure New England air.

Samuel Blodget had fought at Louisbourg and in the French and Indian War, and in the Revolution with General John Sullivan of New Hampshire. He invented a device to raise sunken ships, and he became a judge in New Hampshire's Hillsborough County Court. Then he built a canal around the Amoskeag Falls of the Merrimack River at Manchester, and founded a manufacturing town. He wanted its name to stand for industry in America. "As our country's population increases," he said, "we must have manufactures."

The factories of the Amoskeag Cotton and Wool Company and its subsidiaries grew into the largest manufacturing complex in New England. Miles of walls on both sides of the river encased it as with a canyon of brick.

Francis Cabot Lowell graduated from Harvard and went to England as a rich Boston merchant and studied the methods he saw in the Lancashire cloth mills. He built a power loom for the Boston Manufacturing Company, which he and his brother-in-law Patrick Tracy Jackson, and Nathan Appleton, chartered in 1814 at Waltham, Massachusetts. Their mill was the first in the world to turn raw cotton into finished cloth in one continuous process. The business grew so fast that Jackson bought land in East Chelmsford on the Merrimack River and moved the mill there and named the town that grew up around it Lowell after his partner, who had died. Lowell, Massachusetts, "the spindle city," became one of the world's leading industrial towns.

But it was thirty years before even a jack-of-all-trades New Englander thought out a device to sew up all the cloth the cotton and woolen mills were turning out.

Poorboy Elias Howe left a barren farm in Spencer, Massachusetts, to learn how to make machines in Lowell. Then he went to Boston to learn how to make watches and precision instruments. And he thought and thought about the models of sewing machines other Yankees had built and how to make them practical. Finally Howe saw that if he just put the eye of the needle near its point, and put a shuttle underneath it to form a stitch, he would have solved the problem. In 1846 he got a patent for the result of this flexible thinking, and eventually a place in the American Hall of Fame.

Mill owners nudged shipowners out of the top places in New England society and politics. New Englanders stopped hoisting the sails and climbing the rigging of the merchant ships, and began working the machines of the mills. By the time Elias Howe's sewing machines joined the looms in the factories, the whalers were almost all that was left of New England's seaborne commerce.

The wealth of the whale—oil for the lamps of the world, spermaceti for its candles, bones for women's corsets—had lured New Englanders since the Pilgrims first saw a whale off Plymouth. But the pursuit of leviathan stayed in the offshore waters until well into the eighteenth century, when Nantucket ships began chasing him down the coasts of South America.

Many Nantucket whaling masters were Quakers who had fled to the island from religious persecution in Newburyport. The Revolution put such a crimp in their income from whaling that the Nantucketers are said to have taken in one another's washing to support themselves. Then, with the war over, the whaling masters fitted out their old ships again, and also got new, round-bowed, square-sterned ones built for them. In 1791 they began to venture round Cape Horn into the virtually untapped Pacific, and to plant New England names and ways on its palmy islands.

After the War of 1812 Nantucket's almost total monopoly of whaling was shared with New Bedford, which had a larger, better harbor, road and later railway connections with the interior, and a more vigorous spirit. New Bedford's people, said Ralph Waldo Emerson, "hug an oil cask like a brother."

The Quakers of New Bedford saw the merchant trade dwindling and refitted their cargo ships as whalers. They specialized in whaling. They were shrewd and they made fortunes, but they were also stingy and they were pitiless exploiters. Ninety-eight percent of the profits went to these owners; the crew, who theoretically were paid off by a share ("lay") of the catch, actually were cruelly swindled through tricky accounting. Life on the three-to-four-year whaling voyages was so brutal and vicious, and the skippers could

James Francis Smith, son of a New London whaling captain, 1837. He is wearing a coat made of penguin skins. Like their fathers, boys were now wearing trousers instead of knee breeches (page 71). James later became a ship captain himself.

A whale destroying a whaleboat, as sketched in a ship's logbook.

Whaling off the island of Hawaii, 1833.

be so rascally, that crewmen often deserted to the tranquillity of the South Sea islands. Few ever signed on for a second voyage.

But they had the thrill of the adventure, passing that of any big-game hunter, and the hope of a fortune. No one, wrote Herman Melville, the great romanticizer of whaling in *Moby Dick,* "can feel stranger and stronger emotions than that man does who for the first time finds himself pulling into the charmed churned circle of the hunted sperm whale."

Such fortunes came from whaling that every little seaport of New England south of Cape Cod soon had a fleet of sea hunters. New London, Connecticut, ranked next to New Bedford. Whale products had both a national and an export value, their prices rising to extravagant peaks by 1857, and they made the whaling industry second only to cotton in New England economy.

Then the canny Quakers of New Bedford saw the coming of petroleum and steel. Petroleum would be easier to get and hence cheaper than whale oil; steel would last longer than whale bone. While the commerce of smaller, less specialized whaling ports was expiring, these Quakers were swapping their wind-driven ships for the power-driven spindles of the Wamsutta cotton mills.

A whaler was an ugly ship and awkward, but a clipper clove the waves like a Winged Victory. The clippers were New England's lightning-like response to the challenge of getting forty-niners to the California gold fields before the fever dropped.

A clipper could and did carry cargo. But she was designed and built for speed—sharp in the ends, long in proportion to breadth, and so heavily sparred that when the first New England clipper, *Surprise,* took to the water of Boston Harbor in 1850, guests at the launching were sure she would capsize. She made San Francisco in 96 days, whereas the length of previous trips averaged 160 days.

Her record fell the next year to Donald McKay's *Flying Cloud,* which made it round the Horn to the Golden Gate in 89 days. McKay personally supervised every detail of the clippers he built with such painstaking accuracy that they could log a top speed of twenty-one knots. His clippers were not only fast, they were luxury ships as well.

In spite of their efficiency, the clippers were not profitable. Steam navigation was faster and safer. After six years shipyard owners stopped building clippers. Also, seafaring life had degenerated; it attracted only strong-muscled derelicts and men whom the mills would not employ because of race prejudice. The pay was piddling compared to factory wages, and the risks not worth taking now that a share in the voyage and the chance of advancement were things of the past.

The mills and the factories needed workers. There seemed always to be a place for a new pair of hands weary of plowing and planting and of sharing the small reward with brothers and sisters. The factory whistles played a Pied Piper's tune of regular hours and regular pay, and young New England women especially trooped after it to the mill gates.

Left: Advertisement for the clipper Criterion, *sailing from Boston to San Francisco. Above: Eight-foot figurehead from the clipper* Donald McKay *(1855). The Boston shipbuilder was proud of his Scottish ancestry.*

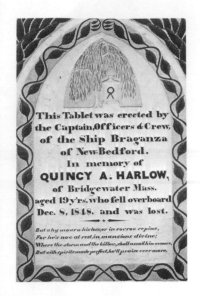

This Tablet was erected by
the Captain, Officers & Crew,
of the Ship Braganza
of New-Bedford.
In memory of
QUINCY A. HARLOW,
of Bridgewater Mass.
aged 19 y'rs, who fell overboard
Dec. 8, 1848, and was lost.

*In the dangerous occupation
of whaling, it was often the
least experienced men whose
lives were lost. The weeping
willow replaced the death's
head (page 91) as a symbol
of mourning in New England.*

William Ellery Channing

Widows, daughters of poor parents, girls left to spinsterhood because the young men were moving West, found a way there to support their children, pay for a brother's education, find a new suitor and earn money for a trousseau to marry him. Sometimes they saved enough of their factory wages to pay off a mortgage on the old farm, or even to make a down payment on a new one, and moved back to the clear air of the green fields and the wooded mountains. Most, however, both men and women, were trapped in six days a week of soul-killing monotony, never seeing the sun except through a grimy window by their machine.

Francis Cabot Lowell had hoped that there would not be in his New England a factory class subjected to horrors like those he had seen in the evil mills of Lancashire. At its own cost his company took pains, he wrote, "in establishing boarding houses . . . under the charge of respectable women, with every provision for religious worship. Under these circumstances the daughters of respectable farmers were readily induced to come into these mills for a temporary period."

Not every mill owner had by any means such pious, virtuous intentions toward his employees. But the "temporary period" was the point. The workers of both sexes were too educated and too intelligent to spend their life mastering just one skill. They moved on to other things. Those who could not and who were exploited by the bosses got recognition of their rights. As early as 1842, the right of workers to combine into a union was legalized by a decision of the Supreme Court of Massachusetts.

The unswerving, intolerant doctrine of the single-minded Puritans had little to say to these people whose well-being depended on their versatility of mind. They were no longer willing to wait for God's justice in the hereafter; they wanted social justice here and now.

William Ellery Channing grew up in beautiful Newport in "godless Rhode Island," as Cotton Mather named it, and in the trees and the sea he felt God quite near him. He studied God's word and he studied new European theories of society, and he could not make them agree with the Puritan way of ignoring a man's material needs and his human feelings. Called to Boston's

Federal Street Church, he preached that a man improves himself by improving the lot of others. The whole duty of man, he said, is to love his neighbor more than himself—a large order, but one that did not daunt New Englanders. They had tamed nature's wilderness, and now they prepared to clean up the mess man had made of man.

They readily followed Channing in his efforts to reform institutions—slavery, labor, prisons—that thrived on hard-hearted injustice. Undeserved suffering, he taught, only makes human beings vengeful and vicious.

New Englanders felt guilty over their prosperity. They examined their Puritan consciences and began changing their communities. For they still were, and they always would be, essentially Puritans, concerned with the common welfare.

Connecticut philanthropists founded private charitable organizations especially designed to aid poor women. In 1816 its legislature granted a charter to Thomas Gallaudet to found a school for teaching the deaf. Dr. Eli Todd fought for funds to establish a hospital

A light-hearted view of a New England schoolroom

D. C. Johnston del.

T. Moore's Lith. Boston.

The George Barrell Emerson School in Boston, about 1850. George was a cousin of Ralph Waldo Emerson.

for humane and scientific treatment of the mentally sick; in 1824 he founded the Hartford Retreat (now the Institute of Living) for the benefit of rich and poor alike. Connecticut's Henry Barnard and Massachusetts' Horace Mann campaigned realistically for improvement of public schools.

Boston's Mayor Josiah Quincy organized the Prison Discipline Society in 1825 after exposing the crime-breeding which existed in jails. Dorothea Dix studied the confinement of the insane "in cages, closets, cellars, stalls, pens, chained, naked, beaten with rods" and got the Massachusetts state insane asylum improved; then she carried her work of reform all over the nation. Dr. Samuel Gridley Howe invented new ways to teach the blind, and for forty years trained teachers for the afflicted at his Perkins Institute.

The ideal of freedom from every kind of bondage—blindness, deafness, mental illness, poverty—was a logical by-product of New England's actual freedom from tyranny. Even women began to be emancipated; Connecticut's Emma Willard and Sarah Porter founded schools for them in Troy, New York, and Farmington, Connecticut.

William Ellery Channing's emphasis on human reason, the heart of man, as the only authority inspired young Ralph Waldo Emerson and Henry David Thoreau to free men from conformity to ideas that did not meet their individual needs.

"Trust thyself," wrote Emerson; "every heart vibrates to that iron string." He would add: "A foolish consistency is the hobgoblin of little minds," meaning that a person torments himself by forcing himself to think in a way that does not suit his nature. He wanted great minds, not little ones. He rebelled against the notion that man is born to sin. The sin, Emerson taught, is not believing in one's own goodness, not following the lead of the spirit, which is in every man as it was in Christ.

Ralph Waldo Emerson

Emerson left his church in Boston because he could not compromise with rules of religion which he did not wholly trust. Relying on his own thoughts and feelings, he lectured in America and England. His addresses, his essays, and his poems influenced a generation to live plainly and think nobly and rely on the pure feelings of a heart warmed and expanded by contemplation of nature's simplicity and order.

Henry Thoreau graduated from Harvard and went back home to Concord and helped his father and brothers in their business of making pencils. One day it occurred to him that for a man to go on making pencils after he had made the best pencil he could make was a waste of man's most important duty. He would not fritter away his life with useless things. His business was to live.

Dorothea Dix

Henry Thoreau went in search of the true aims of life which he felt he had lost—"a hound, a bay horse, and a turtle dove" he once had known but which he had let get away. He borrowed tools from his neighbors in Concord, and built himself a one-room hut in the woods on the shore of Walden Pond. On a Fourth of July he went to live alone there for two years, two months and two days.

There he could be close to nature and learn its lesson of simplicity in which there is no waste. He did not want books—he would only have to dust them, he said—or anything else that would clutter up the life he wanted to simplify. He thought a man

Henry Thoreau's hut, as shown on the title page of his book Walden *(1854)*

Henry Wadsworth Longfellow

can be a slave to things; he does not own them, they own him. Without unneeded things, a man is free to have the life he has consistently imagined. He need not ask himself, in dread of the answer: "What has my life amounted to?" Or, when he comes to death, discover that he has not lived.

When Thoreau found out what he was living for, he left his hut as he had left off pencil-making.

He had no wish to compete for love or money or fame. A man, he thought, is happy merely by satisfying himself. Otherwise he leads a life of quiet desperation—quiet because he does not work to know what he needs, despairing because he does not make his wants simple and wastes his life getting things he does not need. Order is possible only when one does not try to cram too many things into too small a space.

Thoreau also thought it part of man's duty to disobey laws that do not suit his own sense of what is right. Thoreau went to jail rather than pay a tax for the War with Mexico, which he disapproved of.

When Thoreau was dying, a friend asked him if he had made his peace with God. "I did not know we had quarreled," Thoreau said. Life and God to him were one, and he had loved both.

Emerson and Thoreau gathered around them in Concord rebels against the tyranny of a foolish consistency. They were as militant as those who fought and died for freedom at the North Bridge in April's breeze—Bronson Alcott and Nathaniel Hawthorne and Margaret Fuller and Theodore Parker and George Ripley. They lectured and wrote in defense of freedom of the spirit as their ancestors had fired for political freedom.

Thoreau's *Walden* still has meaning for the later twentieth century; it sparked Gandhi to liberate India, and it comforts those trapped in the hurry of competitiveness. And Hawthorne's novel, *The Scarlet Letter,* probes the unhappiness of human beings afraid to follow the lead of their feelings.

The rest of the Concord Group lapsed into misty thinking or into tedious moralizing which the popular versifiers of the time—Henry Wadsworth Longfellow, James Russell Lowell, John Greenleaf Whittier—embedded in rhyme. Moralizing would often turn

New Englanders' earlier practical reforming spirit into pious, meddlesome do-goodism. This kind of reform seldom reached to the cause of distress or deprivation, and so became patronizing rather than constructive charity. After all, nearly every girl was set to stitching into a sampler lines like:

> I slept and dreamed that life was beauty;
> I woke and found that life was duty.

And nearly every boy had to learn:

> Not what we give but what we share,
> For the gift without the giver is bare.

And so on, until a rich and realistic Boston woman of another generation, when asked to contribute to the Charitable Eye and Ear Hospital, quipped: "I didn't know there was a charitable eye or ear in Boston."

Still, she gave to the fund raisers. And so did grumpy Captain Joseph Nickerson, sitting in his chandlery on Boston's India Wharf, longing for the old days when he would dock his *Robin Hood* there and unload her rich Mediterranean cargo. Two timid ladies called on him there for a donation to a home for orphans.

"What d'ye want it for?" he roared as if he were on his bridge in a gale.

"T-to pay off the mortgage," they whimpered.

"Mortgage!" shouted Captain Nickerson. "I don't believe in mortgages! Goodbye!"

Two days later the ladies brought their meager collection to headquarters.

"What in the world did you do to Captain Nickerson?" asked the superintendent. "Yesterday he came here and paid off the whole mortgage."

The orphanage was named for him, and he became very fond of it, and he and his descendants managed it for three generations.

Presently the New England reformers aimed their zeal to improve themselves and their community at a larger target, the institution of slavery in the states of the South.

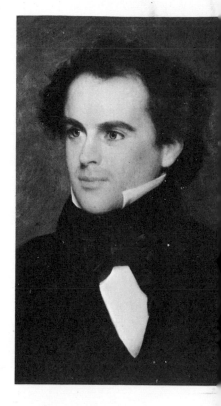

Nathaniel Hawthorne became a close friend of Longfellow, who had been at Bowdoin with him.

On the masthead of the Liberator, *Garrison pictured a slave auction.*

To the New England idealists, compromise with an evil was as much a sin as it was to their Puritan ancestors. Single-mindedness lies under the New England mind, however versatile that mind may be, like the granite under New England fields. It rears out suddenly to shatter the cultivating virtues of patience and wisdom as a boulder crops up to break a ploughshare.

Thinking turned into action when the towns of Maine won independence from the jurisdiction of Massachusetts.

Maine people resented the lack of aid Massachusetts had given them in the War of 1812, when the British seized Maine's towns and bottled up their boats. Then the terrible weather of 1816—"eighteen hundred and froze to death"—when snow in June killed the apple blossoms, and the corn which mittened farmers planted in July was frozen in early September, reduced the region to starvation. Whole communities, as well as hundreds of individuals, moved west to Ohio. Again Massachusetts gave no help, on the principle that each man must look out for himself.

When Maine recovered from this depression there was long agitation for separation from Massachusetts. Some Maine voters opposed it on the grounds that it would mean the end of free trade, and would make the taxes needed to support an independent government too high. Finally, in 1819, Senator Rufus King of New York, who was born in Scarboro, Maine, got a federal law passed guaranteeing free trade in all ports along the Atlantic coast. The separationists won. On March 15, 1820, Maine joined the union as its twenty-third state.

Maine was admitted as a free state. But almost simultaneously Missouri was admitted to the union as a slave state through a political compromise that horrified the New England reformers. The next year, Quaker Benjamin Lundy began issuing his *Genius of Universal Emancipation,* propaganda for the abolition of slavery everywhere in the United States.

William Lloyd Garrison grew up in Newburyport as a poor boy whose revenge for his poverty was a religious conviction that everything the rich did was somehow sinful. He believed that Jesus loved the poor and hated the rich. He learned the printer's trade and went to work on temperance journals and emancipation journals, and went to Baltimore to edit Lundy's paper. He was rabid about the rich slave owners. When he accused two of his fellow Newburyporters of being slave traders, he was sued for libel and convicted, and he served seven weeks of a jail sentence until a sympathizer paid his fine.

The Liberator *also portrayed a joyous scene of Emancipation.*

Then Garrison went back to Boston and got some militant reformers to finance the *Liberator,* a magazine of small circulation which insisted that no compromise whatever with slavery could be morally acceptable. Then he founded the New England Anti-Slavery Society, and soon was the leader of the most extreme reformers. He publicly burned the Constitution of the United States, thus alienating the more moderate anti-slavery people, but the extremists revered him as the leader of a moral crusade to free the slaves.

These people thought freeing the slaves more important than preserving the Union, which the slaveholding states were threatening to dissolve. Daniel Webster maintained that a compromise was possible.

Daniel Webster graduated Phi Beta Kappa from Dartmouth—"a small college," as he said, "but there are those who love it"—and studied law and practiced in the fiercely competitive courts of his native New Hampshire. He was a big man and a proud man and a forceful one. People called him "the God-like Dan'l" and made him a legend in his lifetime. The power of his personality was like Niagara Falls and his integrity was as solid as cloud-wrapped Mount Washington. His face with its deep-set dark eyes —"dull anthracite furnaces," Thomas Carlyle called them, "needing only to be blown"—was as impressive as that of the Old Man of the Mountains, the strange profile nature chiseled out of the granite of New Hampshire's White Mountains at Franconia.

Daniel Webster

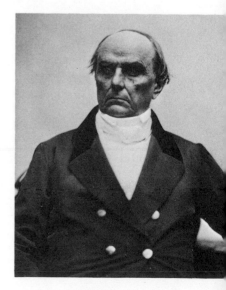

Daniel Webster went to the Supreme Court and argued for the Union according to the Constitution until people called him its "Expounder." He moved to Massachusetts, which sent him to Congress, where in his resounding voice he declared for "Liberty *and* Union, now and forever, one and inseparable." The people of Massachusetts went frantic trying to decide which noble son—

*Expulsion of abolitionists
from Boston's Tremont
Temple in December, 1860*

Garrison or Webster—they ought to follow.

Daniel Webster believed slavery was evil, but he also believed that the federal government had no right to interfere with the internal affairs of the slaveholding states. He thought the breaking up of the Union would be worse than a tolerance of slavery, and he helped to save the Union while he lived.

In 1852 Daniel Webster died on his beloved Marshfield farm. (The last words of that life-hungry giant were, "I still live.") Then there was no strong Northern voice to speak for reason against William Lloyd Garrison's emotional oratory. No one, that is, but an angry Boston mob which almost strung him up on a lamppost —and succeeded only in shocking many moderates into becoming abolitionists. Garrison already had plenty of millhands on his side, factory workers who imagined themselves slaves of the mill owners in Haverhill and Worcester. The mill owners had Garrison stoned because he demanded immediate and unconditional freedom for the slaves of the Southern cotton planters.

Garrison had impassioned propagandists working with him. There was Harriet Beecher Stowe, whose over-emotional novel about maltreatment of the slaves, *Uncle Tom's Cabin,* made its readers weep. And "the good gray poet" John Greenleaf Whittier, who dared denounce Daniel Webster as a traitor to honor and human decency. And Henry Wadsworth Longfellow and James Russell Lowell, who now began to write rabble-rousing verses intended to turn the idealistic New England reformers into gun-toting soldiers. For over a hundred years New Englanders had had good training as propagandists for their causes.

Throughout New England the "Underground Railroad" worked more efficiently than the railways the mill owners had chartered to get their goods to market. At stations of the Underground, runaway slaves were hidden and sheltered and fed and helped on their way to free Canada. New Englanders refused to obey a federal law that required the return of a runaway slave to his owner (the Fugitive Slave Law). They considered that law tyrannical. They had rebelled against the tyrannical laws of nature's wilderness and against the tyrannical laws of England and the tyrannical embargo of Thomas Jefferson and the tyrannical conscriptions of Mr. Madison's War. They were in good trim.

The shots at Lexington and Concord made no more joyous a sound in the ears of righteous New Englanders than the boom of the cannons firing on Fort Sumter. The first states to answer President Abraham Lincoln's call for troops to defend the Union, against which the Southern states had rebelled, were Massachusetts, Connecticut, New Hampshire, Vermont, Rhode Island, and Maine.

Julia Ward Howe was the author of "The Battle Hymn of the Republic," which was widely sung in the North during the Civil War.

Daniel Webster's son led down Boston's State Street a regiment who sang "John Brown's Body." They marched between crowded rows of abolitionists who cheered them on—as it turned out, to death at Bull Run and Chancellorsville and Gettysburg and by Antietam Creek.

Soon the words of their tune would be those of the wife of the Dr. Howe who used his life to teach the blind to "see":

> Mine eyes have seen the glory
>   of the coming of the Lord;
> He is trampling out the vineyard
>   where His grapes of wrath are stored . . .

No one seemed to see very clearly what Julia Ward Howe's words would mean for generations yet to come.

6·THE GILT AND THE GOLD

The Stratford, Connecticut, railroad station in 1867

The dreams of both Daniel Webster and William Lloyd Garrison came true. The Civil War, which began at Fort Sumter, ended with the Union preserved and slavery abolished.

New Englanders felt that they had done a worthy thing in forcing the conflict. The gun factories of Hartford had supplied most of the arms for the victory of the North. The mills of New England had furnished most of the Northern armies' blankets and uniforms. New Englanders believed that they had won the war.

Now they were determined to win the peace. In New Englanders' eyes, only the South was to blame for the cost of the Civil War in money and human lives. It would have to pay for its rebellion against New Englanders' notions of law and order.

Thaddeus Stevens went from Danville, Vermont, to Dartmouth College, and then moved to Gettysburg, Pennsylvania, where he practiced law and made a fortune in real estate and iron. He was sarcastic and he was a shrewd arguer, and after he got to Congress he dominated the newly formed Republican Party. He called for stern measures during the war, and for sterner ones after the South surrendered. And he led the impeachment procedures against President Andrew Johnson, who had hoped to carry out Lincoln's plans for tolerance in reorganizing the Southern states.

New Englanders approved of Stevens' drastic Reconstruction program. Hundreds of them toted their carpetbags into the South, which the war had ruined economically. Some enforced laws and regulations on helpless communities without any understanding of local experiences and conditions or respect for the Southern way of life. Others, however, went to help the Negroes.

Thaddeus Stevens

New Hampshire's General Benjamin Butler had set these carpetbaggers an infamous example of how to deal with a fallen foe by his unchivalrous and stupid humiliation of the people of Louisiana when he was military governor of New Orleans. The Southerners called him "Beast" Butler. President Abraham Lincoln had said: "General Butler is cross-eyed. I guess he don't see things the way other people do."

Neither did many other New Englanders. Later they elected Butler governor of Massachusetts. New England "won" the peace at the cost of having Southerners hate even the word "Yankee" more after the war than they had hated the troops who ravaged their land.

The Civil War brought fantastic sums of money to the owners of New England's factories and mills. In these manufactories lay the real strength New England had shown in the war—or so it seemed on the surface. The owners used their profits to expand their operations. In the years immediately following Lee's surrender at Appomattox, New England's production of shoes and wool and cotton goods led the nation's. New England's shoemaking machinery and paper-mill machinery were world famous. Money poured into the region. Most of it went into the pockets of the factory owners and their few shareholders.

The disastrous Boston fire of
1872 destroyed more than
seven hundred buildings.

In the twenty-odd years since railways made the transportation of goods cheaper, faster, and safer, New England's shipping and shipbuilding had declined. These two great sources of income would soon almost disappear. The fortunes the shipowners and merchants amassed in the eighteenth century were secure; few New England fortunes ever dwindle, owing to New Englanders' extremely cautious investments and the "spendthrift" trusts in which they bequeath their money. But new fortunes were now being made in industry and railroads and the mines of the West.

Many New Englanders invested in the railroads which were linking all parts of the country: the Union Pacific; the Michigan Central; the Chicago, Burlington, and Quincy; the Atchison, Topeka, and Santa Fe. New Englanders were presidents or executives of these lines. The railroads were bringing huge profits to these individuals, but they were making New England itself a more remote and less vital part of the expanding nation than it had been.

New Englanders also organized mining companies, such as

124

Michigan's Calumet and Hecla (copper), and served as executives in them. In comparison with the enormous copper deposits of this mine alone, Vermont's limited supply of copper came to be scarcely worth the cost of mining it.

Hartford became the insurance capital of the country. Insurance as a business in America was another product of Yankees' aggressive cleverness in responding to the challenges of nature. In the late eighteenth century, Hartford merchants combined to share the risks that the ships which carried their goods met from storms, pirates, and wars. The insurers shared the profits of a successful voyage; the losses of an unsuccessful one did not ruin the single merchant who had financed it.

This system worked so well that the insurers formed themselves into companies which undertook other kinds of risks: fire, life, accident in travel, eventually almost all other hazards. New York City's terrible fires of 1835 and 1845, and the catastrophic Chicago fire of 1871, tested the responsibility of these companies and found them strong. From that time on, insurance brought vast sums of money into Connecticut.

A foppish New England undergraduate, as pictured in Frank Leslie's Illustrated Newspaper

The new wealth made its possessors powerful in politics and in society. They assumed the role of aristocrats, but few of them played it well. In a democracy, the only justification for a pretense to aristocracy is leadership on the part of men and women of superior minds who are dedicated to high standards of conduct, who are concerned with the welfare of their society as a whole, who set a tone of unselfish integrity.

The new aristocrats were dedicated to increasing their money. They used their money to ensure the election of legislators who would make no laws that might interfere with the making of more money. They wanted no change in a system which gave them power and kept that power intact. Few showed any responsibility to the workers who made their wealth possible. Few had any concern for the damage their greed was causing society. The tone these self-styled aristocrats set for the period of their rise was completely materialistic.

Generally speaking, the New England participators in the post-Civil War enonomic boom were less guilty of the corruption and graft which made some new fortunes possible than were other manipulators throughout the country. But there were scandals that did include them. Directors of insurance companies, for example, recklessly undertook risks, divided the profits, kept no funds in reserve for inevitable mishaps—and bankrupted their investors.

Mark Twain came out of the West with a fresh eye and a realistic one and a sense of proportion, qualities that made him a great humorist. He had piloted a Mississippi River steamboat, and prospected for silver and gold in the rough mining camps of Nevada and California, and edited a newspaper, and traveled more widely than most Americans, and he was not easily fooled by human behavior.

In 1871 Mark Twain took his gently reared wife to Hartford and built himself a lavish house in Nook Farm, a small community of intellectuals just outside the city proper. Harriet Beecher Stowe lived there, as did her sister Isabella, who was married to a descendant of Hartford's founder, Thomas Hooker. And

Mark Twain lived for twenty years in Hartford, where he wrote Tom Sawyer *and* Huckleberry Finn.

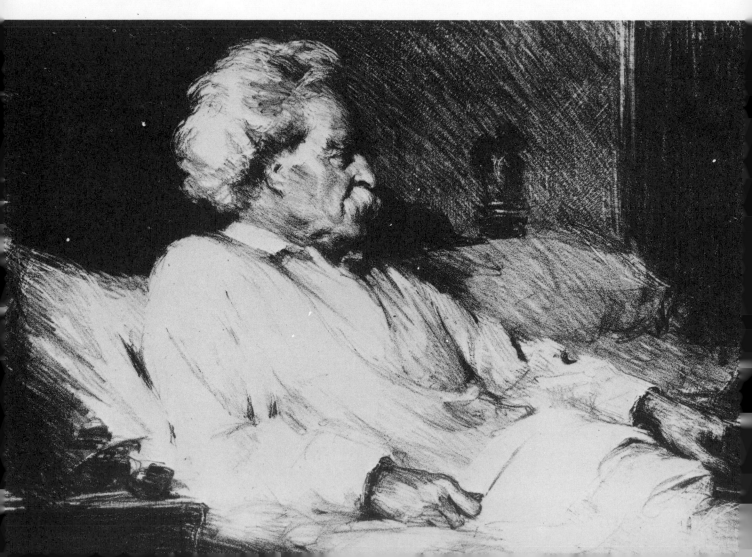

so did a Hartford newspaper owner and editor, Charles Dudley Warner.

Mark Twain hoped that from these high-thinking people he could get for himself some of the refinement he admired in the older New England Way. He found, however, that they wrote for money—as he himself wanted to do—and that they were not true idealists.

Mark Twain called the period "The Gilded Age" to show his scorn for its false values, its corruption and graft, its veneer of elegance. He saw its "morality" as a kind of immorality because the leaders did not consider realities important. Rather, they hid their vulgar chase after material things under a shabby cloak of gentility. Their ideal was to be "genteel." To be genteel meant to ignore any of the main currents of human life—which, if acknowledged, might reveal one's own vulgar share as a human being in the same currents.

Gold in the bank was one thing. Gold of character at that time seemed to be merely gilt paint disguising cheap cast iron.

It was a cast-iron age in many other respects. Impersonal machine-made horrors produced in mass replaced the handwork which had distinguished New England's products ever since Colonial times. Those products—whether the wooden utensils that farm families shaped in the winter or the sturdy tools that New England workmen forged by hand and shipped all over the world —were the work of individuals who loved their craft and were proud of the personal stamp they put on their creations. Machine production of the same articles, especially in the new, cheap process of cast iron, brought prices down and forced handmade things out of the market.

Mass production changed even the appearance of New England. Machine-made things were new, and so they were fashionable. No one seems to have thought them unspeakably ugly. For example, in place of the individualized hand-carved moldings of Bulfinch and McIntyre, ceilings were now sheathed with sheets of metal stamped with the same hideous pattern as the next house and the one next to that—to infinity. Cast-iron "lace" and scroll-saw "gingerbread" appeared on the outsides of houses instead of classical urns and cornices. Vulgar standardization swallowed up much of the individualized dignity of New England living.

Industry brought more and more people from the towns and the country into the cities. The spurt in urban population brought a big building boom.

Hartford blossomed with office buildings copied from Italian examples. Showman P. T. Barnum adorned his native Bridgeport with his own mansion and with public buildings of foreign styles. Boston and Providence began looking like weird composites of medieval and Renaissance European cities.

Architect Henry Hobson Richardson lost his fortune in the wreck which the Civil War made of his native Louisiana, but he scraped up enough money for study in Paris, and he got commissions from burgeoning New England cities. He imposed his version of southern France's Romanesque architecture—which flourished from about the tenth to the twelfth century—on American cities.

Bicycling in Copley Square, Boston, in the 1880's. In the background is Trinity Church, designed in French Romanesque style by Henry Hobson Richardson.

Steerage passengers bidding farewell to Ireland

Richardson designed massive and dignified structures—churches, public buildings, private houses—but he built in red sandstone, not native wood or granite, which emphasized the foreign origins of his work. The smoke of the cities soon smudged these buildings muddy. They seemed to characterize the lack of humor and grace in the life of the period, just as the clean lines of earlier American architects symbolized the reason and proportion of the Federal Period.

A major reason for the industrialists' enormous profits was the low cost of the labor which had become available. Before the Civil War waves of immigration had begun to drop millions of Europeans on American shores. The first of the nationalities to come in great number were the Irish, starting in the 1830's.

It is obvious that in the very beginning every white person in America was an emigrant from Europe. The earlier immigrants to New England, however, were Protestants, many of whom had fled from persecution for their religion as had the first comers. They blended with the founders. The Irish were Catholics.

By 1878 over two and a half million Irish had moved to America. The Cunard Steamship Company had regular sailing schedules between Queenstown, Ireland, and Boston. Its fare was eighteen dollars a head for wretched accommodations. Tens of thousands of Irish, therefore, landed in Boston, and most of them stayed there.

A future American citizen on the dock at Queenstown

They came to escape the neglect they had suffered from absentee landlords in Ireland, or because the Irish potato famine of 1847 had starved them out. They were penniless peasants, unused to the complexity of life in an industrial city. Like animals they burrowed into empty warehouses along Boston's wharves and into cheap sailors' boarding houses and decaying tenements vacant because of the drop in seafaring, and they starved in the land they had heard was one of plenty.

Some of the women became domestic servants, ill paid and often ill treated. The married men took the first jobs they could get. They were uneducated and without skills. Their need for a quick penny sent them to the docks, the railways, or the roads and canals. They worked in muck, and so got the name of "muckers" with all its unsavory overtones.

Others could afford the time and the miserable pay for learning how to operate machines. These went to the factories. They had to take what they could get in the way of wages, and their employers were not generous. Francis Cabot Lowell's provisions for respectable New England farm girls did not apply to the Irish. The

New England factory workers, including women and boys, as drawn by Winslow Homer and engraved for Harper's Weekly *(1868). Homer, who was born in Boston, later lived and worked in Maine.*

workers had to live wherever they might find shelter, not in company-provided, chaperoned boarding houses. A twelve-hour day at a machine was common employment practice, even for children.

The "temporary" quality of the factory jobs native New Englanders took had begun to have meaning. These workers would move on to better jobs or to new areas or back to the farm. Their places were rapidly filled with the foreign-born, who would work for less money and had fewer, if any, ideas of independence. So long as this supply of immigrant workers lasted—and it seemed endless—the products of New England's low-cost industry could undersell those of other regions, even with the expense of shipping raw materials in and finished goods out.

New Englanders despised these unskilled newcomers and gave them small chance to rise in the economic scale, ranking them lower than Negro seamen. The ancient Puritan prejudice against Catholics kept the Irish from responsible jobs they might have filled. Until 1860 it even deprived them of the last rites of their Church when they lay dying in charity hospitals. Boston's Mayor Frederick Prince failed of re-election in 1877 because he had put so many Irish on the police force and thus antagonized his Protestant constituents. Boston ministers preached against the "corrupting" influence of Irish priests and nuns, and a mob burned up a convent.

On the heels of the Irish came Portuguese, Italians, Greeks, Poles and other Middle Europeans, Scandinavians, and Syrians. They were fleeing from oppression and persecution in Europe, or from war and conscription, hoping for freedom and tolerance and peace in America.

These Europeans went to the factory towns and enlarged them into cities. New Haven and Bridgeport in Connecticut, and Lawrence, Lowell, Fall River, Lynn, Brockton, and the other mill centers in Massachusetts teemed with foreign-born factory workers for whom no proper housing or equitable rates of pay existed. In 1870, Connecticut's immigrants were one-fifth of the state's population.

French Canadians, attracted by the work available in the mills of southern Vermont, New Hampshire, and Maine, flocked into towns no better prepared for them than those of Connecticut and

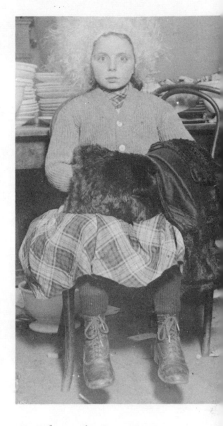

Daughter of a Lawrence textile worker

131

Textile workers on strike in Lawrence, 1912

Massachusetts. Living conditions were hopeless. Disease and crime flourished in slums that swelled like festering growths.

By the early years of the twentieth century, however, the rosy glow of the mill owners had turned gray and chill. The workers had learned to organize into unions. The unions had organized strikes. To keep their machines moving, the owners, who by then had powerful influence in the legislatures, had to grant the demands of their workers. They had to get laws passed to their own disadvantage. No more child labor (in 1887, 1600 children under the age of thirteen, and 153 under the age of nine, were slaving in the factories of Connecticut alone). No more reductions of wages to balance off a slack market, and no more increases in working hours during good market times. The ten-hour day was legalized, and the sixty-hour week. No more blacklisting of workers for belonging to unions and for striking.

The costs of production rose. Furthermore, other regions with greater natural resources than New England could produce most of New England's goods more cheaply and easily. Pennsylvania, for example, with its vast supply of coal and iron and oil, and with

just as great a supply of unskilled immigrant workers, began absorbing New England factories into its industrial syndicates.

Massachusetts state cavalry summoned to clear strikers from the streets of Lawrence

Industries moved nearer the source of supply in order to cut their cost of production. Why ship iron and coal to New England when they were available just outside the walls of a Pittsburgh foundry? Why ship cotton all the way from its source in the South to New England, when mills could be built nearer the plantations in regions that had coal and cheap labor? Or wool from the West, when new industrial complexes were developing much closer to the sheep ranches than New Hampshire and Connecticut? Or hides from Texas for New England's tanneries and shoe factories?

New England, without coal or oil, depended on wood. By the end of the Civil War, New Englanders had already used up most of their wood for fuel for their forges and for heating their houses. Careless deforestation had stripped much of southern New England of the trees that once covered it. What wood had not gone into fireplaces and furnaces went into shipbuilding. The forests in the north were too inaccessible for their lumber to be got out easily and cheaply.

133

The same problem of availability held for New England's small supply of iron. The mines of Salisbury, Connecticut, shut for good; it was too expensive to get their high-grade ore down from the mountains. The miners, isolated and deprived of work, but otherwise unemployable, became inbred derelicts, desperate and sometimes dangerous.

Fishing also declined as a major item in New England's economy. (It did not really revive until the development in Gloucester of new methods of quick-freezing and filleting fish, in the early 1930's.) Fishermen took to easier, less hazardous work in the factories or in trades like gardening, carpentering, and housepainting.

Veterans of the Civil War returned to New England, as had the soldiers of the Revolution, with dreams of a brighter future in the fertile lands they had seen while campaigning. There, endless prairie acres were free for the plowing. Many came home only to pack up and move on. By 1870, some 145,000 Vermonters had left for better chances in the West—almost half the state's population.

Farmers who stuck to their rugged New England fields were gradually ruined by the competition of western agriculture. Farm products could be grown in the West in huge quantity for less money and less labor than in the East. Mechanized farming made sense on the vast farms of the West. The cost of Western produce, even with shipping, was lower than that of Eastern produce. Thanks to the railroads, the West was now feeding the United States.

No state or federal subsidies helped the New England farmers. They had to turn to perishable produce (tomatoes, lettuce, berries, fruits, milk) which could be sold in local markets. In the hot, humid valleys of the Connecticut and Housatonic rivers tobacco proved profitable, but in most other areas the soil was not productive enough to allow the farmers to compete successfully with the rich earth of the West. And the cost of mechanical plows and reapers and binders was too great for the small, stony acres of the New England farmers.

By 1880, western beef production had wrecked New England's beef industry. Butter and cheese production fell off as well. Vermont's few million sheep were no match for the billions in Idaho

and Montana; the Vermonters turned to breeding their famous Morgan horses, and to quarrying their marble and granite. In New Hampshire, forests grew up between the stone walls of abandoned farms.

Parsimony crept into the New England Way. Rural New Englanders' struggles with the land had taught them frugality. Even when they were able to afford luxuries, they chose them of strong materials of relatively permanent value. They justified ornament by confidence that their possessions would last and be useful for generations.

Now that the time was past for more luxuries, country people took such care to keep the ones they had that they got a reputation for stinginess. They liked the wine glasses their parents had got from Boston, not so much for their beauty as for the small amount of wine they held. They saved everything and wasted nothing. Extravagance was a sin to them, worse than the conspicuous waste of the rich.

This attitude of hard-pressed country folk made the urban rich

One of Vermont's special products is the Morgan horse.

135

self-conscious and apologetic. Even well-to-do New Englanders' motto became:

Make it do,
Wear it out,
Use it up,
Or do without!

New Englanders also got a reputation for economy of speech. Not too serious a reason is that the air is too icy for them to keep their mouths open for long at a time. The coast dwellers of Maine, for example, say "ay-ah" for "yes." In the interior, where the winters are colder, the people won't afford two syllables; they say "yup." To New Englanders a waste of words is as wicked as any other extravagance. They tend to think more of how pithily they can utter their thoughts than of how eloquently or graciously. Often the thinking takes them a rather long time, thus increasing their reputation for taciturnity.

Ironically a New Englander, Stockbridge's Cyrus W. Field, made a significant contribution to communication by getting the first transatlantic cable working in 1866. Three years later, another

A public demonstration of Alexander Bell's invention, 1877. In Salem, Massachusetts, Bell spoke into one of his new telephones.

cable, connecting America with France, was pulled ashore in Duxbury and connected with American trunk lines.

Alexander Graham Bell learned to teach the deaf "visible speech" (sign language) in London. He brought his methods to Boston, where he fell in love with one of his deaf pupils. With her inspiring encouragement he finally found a way to make the varying sounds of human speech vary the intensity of an electric current which can, in turn, reproduce the speech. The telephone he thus invented was patented in 1876, and Bell had enough money to marry his pupil the following year.

Hartford was one of the world's first cities to install a telephone exchange, and Mark Twain had the first private telephone installed in his Nook Farm house.

New Englanders could not be passive about the loss of their industries and agriculture to other regions. If it was a cast-iron age, it was also an age of electricity. While the first was ruining the beauty of New England products and houses, the second was providing enterprising Yankees with new outlets for their versatility. A General Electric Company was chartered in Lynn,

At the other end of the line, in Boston, Bell's assistant spoke into another telephone. To be sure the experiment was not a fraud, scientists and reporters made notes of both sides of the conversation.

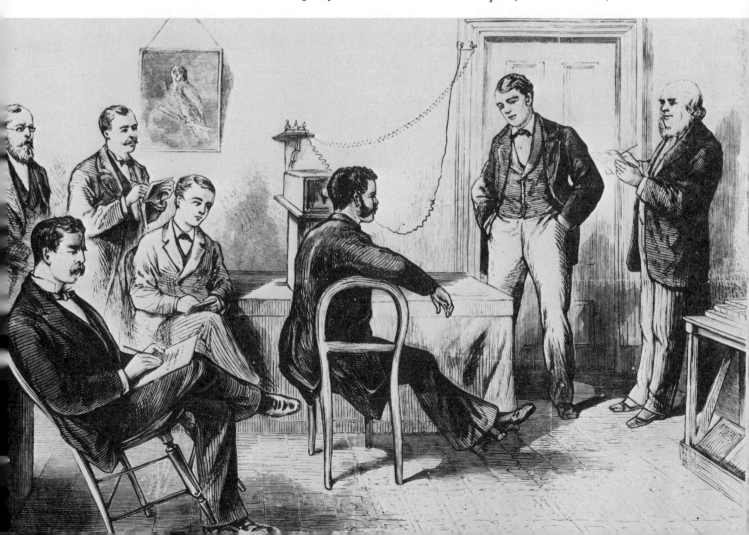

Cyrus W. Field

Made in Springfield, Massachusetts, the Duryea was the first successful gasoline-powered automobile built in the United States. Steered with a tiller, it had a four-horsepower engine with one cylinder.

Massachusetts; and a rubber industry, to provide insulation, in Watertown. Industries that could use the new source of power appeared throughout the region.

Even in the Gilded Age, New Englanders could not wholly forget their intellectual inheritance. Massachusetts Institute of Technology (M.I.T.) opened its doors in 1865. Between that date and 1900 dozens of other educational institutions were founded, many of them designed to train young New Englanders, including women, in the new sciences. Alexander Agassiz used his profits from the Calumet and Hecla mine and from coal mines to found a museum of comparative zoology. Henry Lee Higginson used his fortune from banking to organize the Boston Symphony Orchestra and underwrite its expenses. John Lowell, son of mill owner Francis Cabot Lowell, had left a generous endowment to establish the Lowell Institute in Boston, which gave the public free lectures by leading scholars in every branch of knowledge.

Connecticut's Theodore Gold founded the Storrs Agricultural School, and sparked the establishment of other argicultural colleges to help the farmers recover from their losses to Western agriculture. John P. Norton, a Connecticut farm boy, learned to teach farmers how to apply science to agriculture; his student Samuel William Johnson discovered the use of chemical fertilizers. With Yale's Professor Benjamin Silliman, Jr., they set up a laboratory in New Haven which became the Sheffield Scientific School of Yale University.

At Harvard, William James was exploring human psychology, making discoveries about behavior and attitudes that revolutionized man's treatment of his fellow mortals. Medicine made tremendous progress under Dr. Oliver Wendell Holmes's teaching of anatomy and physiology. Reginald Fitz's diagnosis of appendicitis and his discovery of its cure saved countless lives. They were medical heirs of William Morton, who performed the first operation under an anesthetic in 1846 at Massachusetts General Hospital.

At the same time that New England was losing its economic prestige to other regions, its intellectual prestige was drawing delegations of social planners from the rest of the country to study its educational system, libraries, health departments, and laws. And students from all over the world flocked to its universities.

In spite of the excitement of the period, many New Englanders seemed to wish to withdraw from reality. Material prosperity and the rapidity of change seemed to frighten them. Perhaps they were not prepared for it. Perhaps they thought that they were improving external things at the cost of neglecting improvement of their inner lives.

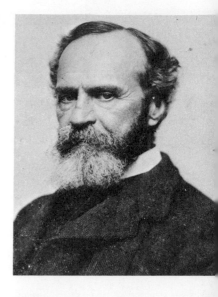

William James

Their Puritan conscience was still strong enough to terrify them at the thought that they might be unable to give a good accounting of the loan of life God had made them. Still strong also was the teaching of the Concord Group. Ralph Waldo Emerson lived until 1882, and was revered as a prophet regardless of his mental decline. The message of those idealists was that happiness meant lifting one's thoughts above material things to the contemplation of spiritual ones. New Englanders of the later nineteenth century tended to become as introspective and self-centered as their Puritan forebears. They acquired thereby a sense of moral and spiritual superiority.

A New England woman who was cultivating her garden on a humid August day was asked whether she did not find the heat oppressive. Mildly but somewhat superciliously she replied: "No, I rise above it"—and went on spading.

Only two of today's religions had their origin in America. Both were established by New Englanders. The Church of Jesus Christ of Latter Day Saints (Mormons) was founded by Joseph Smith, of Sharon, Vermont. Smith, however, left his birthplace when he was ten years old, and had his religious revelation in Palmyra, New York. His church developed principally in the West.

Mary, the youngest of New Hampshire farmer Mark Baker's six children, was a moody girl who threw frightening temper tantrums, and heard otherworldly voices calling her name, and thought she was special. At the age of forty she was so wretchedly neurotic that she went for help to Phineas P. Quimby, who ran an institution of mental healing—a kind of primitive psychoanalysis —in Portland, Maine. Part of the treatment he prescribed for his patients was the study of his book on the power of the mind to cause and cure mental and physical disorders.

Mary Baker Glover Patterson—her first husband died, and she had separated from her second—benefited from Quimby's methods. She thought intensely about his theories and apparently began to relate them to her own meditations on Christ's power to heal.

In 1873 she had a bad fall on the ice. The shock seems to have fused her mental experiences into a workable system of using what she called the "truth" of Christ's divine mind to overcome the "error of human belief" in the reality of all forms of sickness.

This system she called Christian Science. She began to teach its practice to all who would study her discovery, as she called it, of how every human being may make his participation in the reality of the Divine Mind effective in his "dream" of mortal existence.

She married one of her students. Her new name, Mary Baker Eddy, came to mean health and emotional comfort to those who believed in the religion she had founded. The Christian Science Church, which Mrs. Eddy established, does not make public the size of its membership, but it has branches throughout the civilized world, and it must have millions of adherents.

To New Englanders who felt spiritually depressed after the Civil War and who hoped there was more meaning in life than the mere acquisition of material things which they could not take with them, Mrs. Eddy's variations on the New England Way were acceptable. But Christian Science by no means became a dominant persuasion in New England.

In western New England the congregational way still was sturdy, and was being invigorated by the gentle, loving Christianity of Hartford's Horace Bushnell. In Maine and other New England areas where the living is hard, people favored the preaching of Baptists and Methodists. This stressed the eternal reward awaiting those who patiently suffer in their brief earthly years. Emotionally directed sects, derived from these denominations, made self-denial tolerable for northern farmers who saw no escape from grinding poverty. Their tent meetings comfortingly predicted eventual punishment for the pleasures enjoyed by the self-indulgent rich.

Phillips Brooks was descended from Puritan John Cotton and

was related to Congregational Abolitionist Wendell Phillips, but he was brought up as an Episcopalian. He became a priest, and eventually a bishop of the Episcopal Church. He preached from Boston's Trinity pulpit that the intellectual values of the persisting Puritan beliefs would grow stronger if mixed with the glad spirit of early Christianity. This charitable, tolerant spirit he himself offered. Phillips Brooks had an irresistibly winning personality, and he preached eloquently, and he snapped his congregations out of their withdrawal from reality into constructive, realistic living.

The Old Meeting House (Baptist) at Sandwich, New Hampshire

141

On a visit to England, young Reverend Endicott Peabody sensed the spiritual vigor in schools like Dr. Thomas Arnold's Rugby. When Peabody came home to Boston, Phillips Brooks urged him to copy these schools in one of his own. Peabody started this at Groton, Massachusetts, for boys to live together and practice a "muscular Christianity" of the Episcopalian variety.

Groton was not the first of the Episcopalian schools in America designed to prepare boys for life first and college second; St. Paul's in Concord, New Hampshire, preceded it by some thirty years, and there were others. Groton School, however, set a standard of uncompromising mental, moral, and physical training that was widely imitated.

Public-school education in New England had by no means declined. In fact, the curriculum of public schools had broadened far beyond the old classical training and now included courses in physics, chemistry, biology, geography, manual training and domestic science. The states set up high schools for teaching industrial, agricultural, and business techniques. Private gifts established other schools which specialized in one sort of vocational training or another for both young men and young women.

Independent education, however, became one of New England's industries. The old free town academies revived as exclusive boarding schools, and the Gothic spires of their new chapels shared the skyline with the steeples of the old meetinghouses.

Not all these schools followed the "St. Grottlesex" (St. Paul's-Groton-Middlesex) pattern. Ancient Phillips Andover and Exeter, for example, remained non-denominational, and Milton and Hotchkiss are perhaps more Unitarian than anything else. But they are alike in a kind of holy thoroughness. This, and the cost of attending them, attracted the sons of conscientious New England families and also boys from sections of the country which New Englanders had settled. The New England Way, as it were, came back to the factory for reconditioning, then went forth again with shiny new efficiency.

An education at one of New England's "prep" schools came to be as much in demand as the products of New England's other machines once were. A flaw in that product was that in their earlier years many of those educational institutions were not genuinely American. They copied English models. Nor did they truly represent American individualism and democracy. They aimed at producing aristocrats, and sometimes they did, but they also helped produce a class of New Englanders who considered themselves superior beings, arrogant and autocratic.

New England's physician-poet-humorist Oliver Wendell Holmes, Sr., called the members of this class "Brahmins," a term he borrowed from the highest caste in India's old rigid social system. A Brahmin's value to society as a whole is purely intellectual. He does not work; rather he has to be supported by the lower castes. He does not earn his rank in any way; he is born into it. Thus he is a burden on the rest of society, an ornament of no practical value. And he has no contact whatever with those who maintain him as a dubious example of spiritual superiority.

The few drops of this new element of New England society—the Brahmins were a small group—colored the whole, and the part has often been mistaken for the whole. The Brahmin became a myth. Like all other myths, this one soon acquired a semi-divine nature. This aspect of the myth commanded respect and reverence from the superstitious.

The Brahmins were supposed—and supposed themselves—to be intellectuals. Actually they were bookish and unimaginative, plowing over the ideas of others as their ancestors plowed the fields until the soil gave a meager yield.

Brilliant Oliver Wendell Holmes, Jr., fought in the Civil War, and studied law, and listened to William James explain his discoveries about human nature. Young Holmes was engaged to teach in the Harvard Law School. In 1881 he was invited to give a series of lectures at the Lowell Institute. He shocked his audience, especially the conservative lawyers in it, by announcing—and demonstrating—that the Common Law is based on experience, not logic.

This new theory caused his published lectures, *The Common Law,* to be banned from at least one famous law library. But Holmes went on teaching, especially influencing a favorite pupil who was an immigrant German Jew from Kentucky, Louis D.

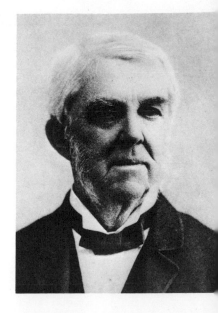

Oliver Wendell Holmes of the Harvard Medical School (above) was a popular writer and poet. His son of the same name (below) went from the Harvard Law School to the Massachusetts Supreme Court, and then to the U.S. Supreme Court.

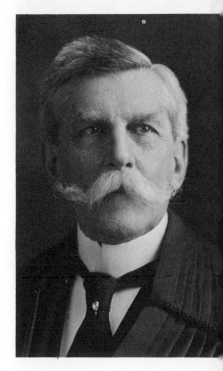

Brandeis. Both would be heard from later in their long lives, and both would establish in America a new liberal concept of law and its relation to human needs, human life, and human freedom.

The banning of books was part of New Englanders' deliberate self-isolation from a world they thought too crude for them. The Concord Free Library banned Mark Twain's *Huckleberry Finn* from its shelves as soon as the novel was published in 1885. Mark Twain's reaction, like that of many another author of a New England-banned book, was that this censorship would help sales. The librarians thought *Huckleberry Finn* immoral, failing to see that Huck's moral code is a plea for tolerance and against oppression. Huck, possibly the most realistic and lovable boy in all literature, they thought wicked because he smoked and lied (to save a friend) and associated with irresponsible characters. Certainly he was no good example for genteel New England boys to follow.

Freedom of expression and genuine emotion were thought improper by these imitation Puritans. They hid their real feelings, and protected their emotional privacy as they did their wealth. In Amherst, timid, wren-like Emily Dickinson never showed anyone the exquisite poems she distilled from her poignant feelings. She seldom went outside her father's house, and she shrank from visitors, and to keep her heart's privacy inviolate she stowed away the scraps on which she had written such quietly passionate lines as:

Emily Dickinson

> I never hear the word "escape"
> Without a quicker blood,
> A sudden expectation,
> A flying attitude.
>
> I never hear of prisons broad
> By soldiers battered down,
> But I tug childish at my bars—
> Only to fail again!

Emily Dickinson's New England contemporaries would have preferred such banalities as Longfellow's:

> Into each life some rain must fall;
> Some days must be dark and dreary.

144

In other ways, too, the Brahmins were inverted snobs. They self-consciously underplayed their wealth and education so as to appear modest and even humble. On the streets they wore clothes they bought at bargain basements; at their own parties they wore dresses from Worth in Paris and suits tailored on London's Savile Row. Their carriages and houses were shabby outside, luxuriously overstuffed inside.

They hired the technically gifted, stylish John Singer Sargent to preserve their external features on canvas, as their ancestors had commissioned Copley and Stuart to paint portraits of their souls. Their own lack of inner creativity suited Sargent's own. They also commissioned Sargent to decorate their public buildings with pious high-Episcopalian murals.

The Brahmins hated any other form of pretense, even aids to personal beauty. They were ruthlessly honest in their opinions, and often offered them without being asked. They were also scrupulously honest about money; their dread of debt sometimes kept them from expanding projects. They played sporting games and spent fortunes on racing yachts and polo ponies, but they never gambled. They trained themselves rigorously to win as amateurs in

John Singer Sargent's portrait of the daughters of Edward D. Boit of Boston. This is one of Sargent's finest paintings.

Henry James, photographed in Newport at the age of seventeen

tennis and golf and ice-skating, but scorned to compete outside their own clubs.

They denied themselves pleasures. They punished themselves with Spartan fare. A European dining at James Russell Lowell's house sniffed the creamed dried codfish that was being offered him and asked if he might be permitted to "omit the fish course." Hungrily he discovered that no other dish was to be served. Saturday night's baked beans were eaten cold on Sunday morning—"to save it." Oatmeal was compulsory at every breakfast, though at least one Brahmin broke down and confessed that he had never liked it.

They associated only with one another, thus inspiring the irreverent verse about Boston and two of its "proper" families:

> Here's to dear old Boston,
> The home of the bean and the cod,
> Where the Lowells speak only to Cabots,
> And the Cabots speak only to God!

The Brahmins found little to cherish or copy in contemporary America. They thought its standards were vulgar, and turned to Europe for models. William James's brother Henry, the outstanding novelist of the period, half-respectfully and half-mockingly pictured their conflicts in Europe between their narrow sense of responsibility and duty and their wish to appear as casual and sophisticated as Europeans. Henry James eventually forsook Boston to live as a British citizen in England's older and wiser atmosphere.

In Newport, about 1904

The self-isolation of the New Englanders was partly due to invasion by "summer people." Newport had long been a summer resort for Americans who lived inland or in less pleasant climates. The depression of the War of 1812 closed Newport's mills, and since it had never been a whaling port, it found catering to these summer residents an adequate substitute for industry.

From New York and Pennsylvania and Illinois came families whose fortunes were expanding to royal proportions through the development of coal and oil and the railroads. They built themselves "cottages" of palatial size and grandeur, and held such court

146

in them that Newport became synonymous with the showy elegance of a society built on wealth alone.

The best American architects were hired to design these palaces. So heavy was their dependence on European models, however, that nineteenth-century Newport, for all its magnificence, looked ridiculous in its New England setting of rocks and the sea.

Almost the same kind of development took place on Maine's mountainous Mt. Desert Island, and in Lenox, Massachusetts, in the Berkshire Hills. Huge rambling hotels blotched the Maine coast and New Hampshire's White Mountains for the accommodation of summer visitors who could afford their rates yet did not wish the encumbrance of a mansion. Rich refugees from overcrowded New York City infiltrated the southwestern portion of Connecticut and gradually turned it into a super-suburb of Manhattan Island.

The self-consciously simple New Englanders looked with disgust at the desecration of their rugged countryside by the vulgar display of these invaders. The rural folk were glad enough to profit from

The Breakers is a 70-room palace on the shore at Newport. It was built for a New Yorker, Cornelius Vanderbilt II.

*Franklin Pierce,
fourteenth President of the
United States, was born in
Hillsboro, New Hampshire.*

*Chester A. Arthur,
born in Fairfield, Vermont,
became the twenty-first
President of the United States.*

the business the summer people brought, but had no more respect for them than the "proper" city people had. The outsiders bought too much and worked too little to please New Englanders, who, if they went away at all in summer, studiously kept their modest summer houses weatherbeaten and ramshackle and congruent with the rough landscape.

The resentment New Englanders felt toward intruders was part of their inheritance from the Puritans who wanted no corruption of their "city upon a hill." It caused New Englanders to withdraw socially from the life of the nation as they had tended to withdraw mentally from the distractions of realities.

A proper Bostonian once asked a friend setting out for the West whether he was going "by way of Dedham" fourteen miles away. (The question has been irreverently misinterpreted; for centuries the "Dedham Road" was the major highway from Boston westward, and Dedham was the first stage on it.) But a proper Bostonian woman replied to a suggestion that she take a trip: "Why should I travel when I am already here?" Boston was to them "the hub of the universe," as Dr. Holmes facetiously called it. Actually it was only a regional capital.

When a proper Bostonian spoke of "the President," he was referring to the president of Harvard University. New England had had bad luck with the men it sent to the White House. John Adams and his son John Quincy Adams were able, almost great statesmen, but they were poor politicians. Both father and son lacked talent for choosing advisers wisely, and neither understood political figures from other parts of the nation, or their motives. They and their descendants were stronger in Congress and in the embassies and government departments they served.

New Hampshire's Franklin Pierce had been President for one miserable term. Vermont's Chester A. Arthur could not control his Congress. The national electorate came to distrust New Englanders, as New Englanders distrusted other Americans who saw little merit in qualifications of birth and education alone.

Politically this small class of New England Brahmins were still Federalists at heart, believing in a government by wise, educated men and in the protection of private property, especially their own.

It was too antiquated a policy to cope with the social revolution going on right under their nose. Yet they held control of politics in New England for a long time under the party name of Republicans.

The Irish had kept coming to New England, lured, like the Pilgrims, by shipping companies' exaggerated advertisements of the opportunities awaiting them in the land of the free. By 1899, there were 225,000 Irish in Boston alone.

The earlier arrivals had found that their only opportunity was in politics. Whenever a new shipload of Irish immigrants arrived from Queenstown, an Irish ward boss was on the Boston dock, ready to help his fellow countrymen keep out of the poorhouse in exchange for their vote. The Irish organized. Through politics they began to attack the conservative Brahmins who persisted in

Boston city election in 1888. Women could not vote in United States national elections for thirty-two more years.

ignoring their needs. Many of the once-immigrant Irish were by now second-generation New England citizens. They had learned the right and duty of rebellion against tyranny.

James Michael Curley was born in Roxbury in 1874, the year, he said, in which the dome of the Boston State House was gilded. His parents were an Irish scrubwoman and an Irish hod carrier. It did not take him long to learn, as he wrote in his autobiography, "that as far as Boston was concerned, liberty was in the clouds; fraternity, nowhere; and equality, beneath the earth"—for an Irishman. And he learned from Martin Lomasney, boss of Boston's Ward Eight, that politics was the only way in which that situation could be changed.

Curley was strong and handsome, and he was witty, and he had a gift for juicy eloquence. By the time he was twenty-six years old he had made his Irish constituents enough promises for them to elect him to the Boston Common Council. Ten years later he was in Congress and, three years after that, mayor of Boston.

Curley declared war on the Brahmins and their Good Government Association—he called them the "Goo-goos"—who tried to keep things as they were. He exposed their self-interest, threatened them, used innumerable imaginative political tricks both honest and questionable to beat them at the polls. He got himself elected mayor of Boston three more times, and governor of Massachusetts once. By the time he had lost to rival Irish politicians, the Irish were in control of Massachusetts politics and, to a lesser degree, of Connecticut politics as well.

Curley's opponent was often another Irish-American with similar tactics—John F. ("Honey Fitz") Fitzgerald, also a mayor of Boston. He lived to see his grandson John Fitzgerald Kennedy elected to Congress, but he died before the same grandson became the thirty-fifth President of the United States.

In spite of a certain amount of opportunism, always a part of politics, Curley brought Massachusetts many benefits both physical and ideological. He foresaw that local and national government would have to become more socialistic in order to serve its millions of citizens.

James Michael Curley served as Boston city councilman, U.S. congressman, mayor of Boston, and governor of Massachusetts.

Curley was cordially hated by New Englanders who still clung to one or both of these guides. Eventually the Brahmins defeated him. In their complacency they failed to recognize that human history is, like the wilderness their ancestors had tamed, a dynamic force demanding aggressive responses to its aggressive challenges. They had forgotten, or perhaps never learned, to reverence what Thoreau called "the miracle of change."

John F. Fitzgerald posing proudly with his wife and children for a family portrait. At far right is his daughter Rose, who married Joseph P. Kennedy.

7 · FROM MYTH TO MIRACLE

Back Bay, Boston New Englanders wandered into the twentieth century with no clear sense of where they were or of where they were going. The New England Way seemed to have forked in several directions. They were puzzled as to which one they should follow.

Henry Adams had the detached mind of a great historian, but as a person he was involved with the fate of his native region and of his country. His father, an ambassador to Great Britain, had kept England from recognizing the Confederacy during the Civil War, and Henry had been his secretary. Henry's grandfather had been President of the United States and afterward "the old man eloquent" of the United States Senate. His great-grandfather had steered the American Revolution to victory and, as second President of the new republic, had kept the nation on an even keel. For over sixty years Henry Adams had swum in the mainstream of America's political and social life. Now Henry Adams was baffled.

In 1907 he had his autobiography, *The Education of Henry Adams,* privately printed. He let only sympathetic friends read it, for he was frightened at his own pessimistic conclusions and depressed by the thought that his life had been a failure. He recognized that because of his disgust at the course of American life during his mature years, he had been only a spectator at a gaudy, senseless, disorderly pageant.

The public did not read Henry Adams's autobiography until 1918. They caught its mood as they were catching the influenza which swept in an epidemic over America and over New England particularly. The *Education* became one of the most influential books of the twentieth century.

Alert New Englanders recognized that they had been worshiping false gods—the myths of the Brahmins. But with the majority the tradition had become a superstition. They felt about following the established way as a fearful person might feel about walking under a ladder or laying a hat on a bed. Better not change just in case . . .

Even after the horror of World War I had made less superstitious people question old values, New Englanders clung to theirs.

Massachusetts' Senator Henry Cabot Lodge was a Brahmin, and he had been an intimate friend of President Theodore Roosevelt and President William Howard Taft. He had supported President Woodrow Wilson's war policies, even though Wilson was a Democrat and progressive and visionary. Lodge was a conservative Republican.

Charles Francis Adams was the son and grandson of United States Presidents (page 92).

Henry Adams, son of Charles Francis Adams, at the time of his graduation from Harvard.

153

One of Boston's non-striking policemen, conferring with a guardsman

Wilson came back to Washington from the Peace Conference at Versailles, where he believed he had learned what the rest of the world needed and wanted in order to prevent another holocaust. Wilson proposed to Congress that America join the League of Nations, the peace-keeping organization which he had urged the Conference to set up.

Henry Cabot Lodge turned his personal prejudice against Wilson into a fight to keep America out of the League. The message of George Washington's Farewell Address, that America should beware of foreign entanglements, was over a hundred years old. The context had completely changed, and Washington's meaning had changed with it. But the tradition had become a superstition. Lodge fought Wilson's plans and got them defeated.

The corruption that followed World War I did not bypass New England, for all the mythical morality of its citizens. Republican Party boss J. Henry Roraback dominated Connecticut politics. Graft was to make the construction of Connecticut's Merritt Parkway a national scandal. Massachusetts wallowed in political corruption and graft under ineffectual leaders.

Calvin Coolidge had a dry New England wit. When he was an undergraduate at Amherst College, there was a student fracas in which a stove was bounced downstairs with a frightful racket and considerable damage to the fraternity house in which Coolidge was sleeping upstairs. When asked why he had paid no attention and had not tried to stop the riot, Coolidge replied: "Wasn't my stove."

When he went into politics from Northampton, his backers told him to keep his mouth shut—humor was no asset in politics. Coolidge almost always did whatever he was told to do. He got to be governor of Massachusetts, and he got to be known as "Silent Cal."

While he was in office, 1117 of the Boston police force of 1544 men struck for better wages (they had been getting only $1100 per year for twelve-hour shifts), cleaner station houses, more sensible uniforms, and the right to unionize. For two September days in 1919, Boston experienced mob rule like that of Sam Adams' Sons of Liberty. Brahmins and Harvard students put on their war uniforms, if they had them, were issued police badges and revolvers, and directed traffic. Otherwise there was no one to replace the

strikers, and the strikers were encouraging criminals.

To the American Federation of Labor, to which the police had applied for a union charter, Coolidge sent a message: "There is no right to strike against the public safety by anybody, anywhere, any time." Then he called out the Massachusetts state guard.

President Wilson congratulated Governor Coolidge on his action. Coolidge's smug maxim got him elected to the vice-presidency of the United States.

Old Senator Henry Cabot Lodge, still alarmed by anything foreign, viewed the Boston police strike as an attempt on the part of the Bolsheviks to sovietize America. But 1919 was a year of strikes throughout the country. In that time of primitive labor legislation, strikes were the only way in which workers could get recognition of their rights.

Lodge and other conservatives kept many people in a state of panic over changing events. They believed that these changes were threatening all security, instead of merely extending security to all classes. Scarcely anyone paid attention to experiments on a farm

Massachusetts state guard called out by Governor Calvin Coolidge to suppress the police strike

155

Governor Coolidge at his desk during the police strike. Later he became the thirtieth President of the United States.

in Auburn, just outside Worcester, that would change man's place in the universe.

Robert Hutchings Goddard always was fascinated by the possibilities of flight into space. By the time he was twenty-five years old and had graduated from Worcester Polytechnic Institute, he had recorded theories about rockets that proved to be fifty years ahead of their time. He even projected manned round-trip flights to the planets. In 1919 the Smithsonian Institution published the results of the tests Goddard made with solid-propellent rocket motors, *A Method of Reaching Extreme Altitudes*.

The Smithsonian gave Goddard financial support. Goddard went on to work with liquid fuels. On March 16, 1926, he launched his liquid-fuel model rocket. This was the first practical step toward the space age which would liberate man from confinement to earth alone.

President Theodore Roosevelt had called Oliver Wendell Holmes, then Chief Justice of the Supreme Court of Massachusetts, to the Supreme Court of the United States. President Wilson called Louis Brandeis to the Supreme Court, an appointment that shocked the traditionalists—for Brandeis was not only a Jew but a liberal who had dared to represent the workers against the employers in Massachusetts and had won important rights for them.

These two Justices fought for the freedom the Constitution assures to every citizen of the United States. Holmes got the title of "The Great Dissenter" because of his many disagreements with the majority decisions of the Supreme Court. The Court tended to put very strict interpretations on the right of free speech guaranteed in the Constitution. Holmes and Brandeis would decide that the freedom of the individual was more important than the sanctity of a tradition.

A worker named Abrams and his associates had published two leaflets protesting the proposed intervention of the United States to suppress the Bolshevik revolution in Russia. The Supreme Court upheld their conviction for this possibly seditious act, and their prison sentences of twenty years. Holmes read one of his most famous dissenting opinions:

156

I believe the defendants had as much right to publish as the Government has to publish the Constitution of the United States now vainly invoked by them. . . . When men have realized that time has upset many fighting faiths, they may come to believe even more than they believe the very foundations of their own conduct that the ultimate good desired is better reached by free trade in ideas—that the best test of truth is the power of the thought to get itself accepted in the competition of the market, and that truth is the only ground upon which their wishes can be carried out. That, at any rate, is the theory of our Constitution. It is an experiment, as all life is an experiment.

Robert Goddard and his associates after a successful rocket experiment in Auburn, Massachusetts, near Worcester

Thus the older New England Way found a voice in the capital of the nation—one which came from the ultimate authority of its law. But in New England itself, even Massachusetts' reputation for justice, famed since John Adams defended the British soldiers involved in the Boston Massacre, got sadly tarnished.

On April 15, 1920, in South Braintree, Massachusetts, a paymaster and his guard were carrying the cash they intended to distribute to the employees of two shoe factories. The men were shot and killed. On May 5, Nicola Sacco, a home-loving pieceworker, and Bartolomeo Vanzetti, a poor fish peddler, were arrested and charged with the murders.

The accused were immigrant peasants from Italy who could barely speak English—"nameless, in the crowd of nameless ones," Vanzetti called himself. They were "anarchists," as workers who

Bartolomeo Vanzetti (left) and Nicola Sacco, handcuffed in court, anxiously awaiting sentence. During his years in prison, Vanzetti learned English well enough to write eloquently about his beliefs.

agitated for better conditions were termed in those days of abject fear of change. The fear found an outlet—a scapegoat like the derelicts of Salem who were hanged for witchcraft—when Sacco and Vanzetti went on trial before Judge Webster Thayer in Dedham from May 31 to July 14, 1921.

Judge Thayer was a butcher's son from Worcester. He had worked his way up in the world. He was short, and he was excessively vain, and he had little self-confidence. He distrusted all foreigners, and he hated anarchists because they interfered with the peace and prosperity of the rich men whose friendship Judge Thayer courted.

The actual evidence against Sacco and Vanzetti was slight. Both men had good alibis. Judge Thayer, however, seems to have let his personal prejudice govern his decisions on what evidence the jury should consider. He publicly expressed his biased opinions, a serious breach of legal ethics. The jury found Sacco and Vanzetti guilty.

Violent protests against the verdict came from liberal jurists, leading intellectuals, and labor sympathizers all over the world. Professor Felix Frankfurter of the Harvard Law School published in the conservative *Atlantic Monthly* an article (later a book) denouncing Judge Thayer, the jury, the witnesses, and the verdict. Justice Oliver Wendell Holmes agreed with Frankfurter that "the case was tried in a hostile atmosphere." From England, H. G. Wells gave perhaps the neatest estimate of the verdict: "the self-righteous unrighteousness of established people."

The verdict was appealed, but upheld. Petitions deluged Governor Alvan T. Fuller of Massachusetts to set aside the sentence of death that Sacco and Vanzetti received on April 9, 1927. Rich Governor Fuller knew how to sell Packards, but he believed the death penalty kept crime down, and he had no notion of how to deal with a situation that had become an international scandal.

Governor Fuller hesitated to reprieve the two men in the death house of Charlestown jail. Boston filled with angry intellectuals and outraged proper New Englanders. They picketed the State House, the governor's house, the prison. One Bostonian lady, arrested for thus disturbing the peace, was furious at being only fined two dollars and sent home; she wanted to go to jail with the more violent demonstrators. Boston was under heavy police guard. There were riots in other cities.

Fuller was unwilling to take single responsibility for commuting the sentence. Finally he announced that his advisers had counseled him against doing so.

Sacco and Vanzetti were electrocuted on the night of August 23, 1927.

After forty years, the truth seems to be that Sacco may have been guilty, that Vanzetti was innocent, that both had been unfairly tried. From his death cell, Vanzetti wrote:

> If it had not been for this thing, I might have live out my life talking at street corners to scorning men. I might have die, unmarked, unknown, a failure. Now we are not a failure. This is our career and our triumph. Never in our full life can we hope to do such work for tolerance, for joostice, for man's onderstanding of man, as now we do by an accident.

When President Warren G. Harding died suddenly in August, 1923, Cal Coolidge took the oath of office in the parlor of his farmhouse birthplace in Plymouth, Vermont. His father, whom he was visiting, administered the oath by lamplight. The scene led Americans to imagine that homespun Cal would be another Abe Lincoln, but Cal did little in the White House—and said less. The country raced along through unprecedented prosperity and corruption. It reached inevitable ruin two years after Cal had said, "I do not choose to run" (for a second presidential term), and retired from public life.

The Great Depression, which began with the stock market crash of October, 1929, completed the ruin of most of the New England industries which had begun to decline in the 1880's. Woolen and cotton mills, in particular, had not kept pace with advances in manufacturing processes. The owners retained and kept hiring low-cost workers too unskilled to cope with new methods and new machines. The factories could not survive the loss of their markets due to the nationwide poverty.

By 1936, the enormous Amoskeag mills of Manchester, New Hampshire, had collapsed, throwing 15,000 people out of work and paralyzing the state's largest city. In New Bedford, Taunton, and Fall River, Massachusetts, half the workers lost their jobs as the textile mills and industrial plants closed down. Mighty Lawrence and Lowell suffered as much. Cities defaulted on their bonds, adding bankruptcy to poverty.

In Connecticut, forty to fifty percent of the textile-center workers were jobless. Hunger marchers had descended on Hartford and forced the legislature to give the unemployed and their families $12,000,000 in direct relief. It was impossible for the local communities in New England to care for their hungry citizens in the traditional ways through public and private welfare agencies. All the Connecticut legislature could think of doing was to raise taxes and impose new ones.

New Englanders seemed determined to deal with their problems in their old independent way. They wanted no interference from the federal government, which, under President Franklin D. Roosevelt, was greatly aiding other regions with its measures of relief. New Englanders thought these measures high-handed. The Brahmins resented the socialism of Roosevelt's New Deal policies as a threat to their prosperity. Roosevelt had recognized Soviet Russia, a sure sign to isolationist New Englanders that he was leading the country toward communism.

Democrat President Roosevelt was snubbed by other alumni, Republicans, at a Groton School commencement. At the celebration of the three hundredth anniversary of his alma mater, Harvard College, he was snubbed by university officials as well.

Later in that same year of 1936 came the climax of New Englanders' withdrawal from national policies, their apathy to national problems, their indifference to the international scene. Maine and Vermont were the only two states in the Union which did not give their electoral votes to President Franklin D. Roosevelt. It is said that at one point on the Vermont border a sign read: "You are now leaving the United States and entering Vermont."

On top of all other miseries came the hurricane of September, 1938, which destroyed billions of dollars in property and took hundreds of lives throughout southern New England and northward into Vermont.

There were plenty of not-so-proper New Englanders who cared little about what their Brahmin non-employers might think of Roosevelt and his successful program of recovery. Jobless workers swung their states to support him. Bridgeport, Connecticut, even elected a Socialist mayor, Jasper McLevy, who came close to winning the governorship of the state. The reality of the Depression killed the myth of the Brahmins.

After the devastating hurricane of 1938, the boats and piers of New London looked like a giant game of jackstraws.

World War II brought economic recovery. New Englanders had learned not to concentrate so heavily on a few forms of industry. They noted that even in the worst times of the previous ten years their production of electrical machinery and metalwork and ready-made clothing had increased. They saw that the cost of new techniques, better management, labor-saving devices, and higher wages for more skilled workers would be outweighed by the greater value of new products.

By the end of the war new industries had taken over abandoned textile factories: synthetic fibers, artificial leather, molded rubber, electrical and electronic apparatus, airplanes (later jets), helicopters, chemicals—all proceeding from the new scientific research called technology.

The Protestant ethic had died with the myth of the Brahmins. It was clear that one could not work hard when there was no work to be had. A new ethic was born—the responsibility of a government to all its people, of that people to one another and to other peoples.

President Charles W. Eliot of Harvard University, one of America's foremost educators, died on the same day of 1926 as film star Rudolph Valentino. In that era of perverted values, even the Boston newspapers gave little space to Eliot's career, so full were they with tributes to the idol of countless American women. Eliot had observed that the public needs seventeen years to get accustomed to a new idea. It was exactly seventeen years from the time the stock market crash of 1929 induced the Great Depression until the new ethic induced Massachusetts voters to send 31-year-old John Fitzgerald Kennedy to the House of Representatives.

Six years later, Kennedy ran successfully for the United States Senate against Henry Cabot Lodge, Jr. "It was those damn teas that licked me," Lodge said in reference to the political parties Kennedy's women supporters gave. The tone of New England politics had changed from the campaigns of "Honey Fitz," when rallies often ended in brick-throwing riots, to an atmosphere of proper receptions at fashionable hotels.

Hatred of the Irish and prejudice against Catholics were as good as dead in Boston. Kennedy, descended from an Irish immigrant saloonkeeper and a grocer, in other respects had the qualifications of a proper Bostonian—a rich family, education at a New England prep school (Connecticut's Choate), and a degree with honors from Harvard.

In his inaugural address as President of the United States, Kennedy said: "Ask not what your country can do for you—ask what you can do for your country."

Kennedy invited Robert Frost to speak a poem at the inauguration. It was the first time in history that a poet had been so honored or that any official recognition had been given the arts on such an occasion.

Some sixty years earlier this 85-year-old poet had returned from his birthplace in California to his father's native New England. He had made New England—where he finally settled in Ripton,

John F. Kennedy with his wife and daughter, at their summer house in Hyannis-port, Cape Cod. This photograph was taken on the day he was elected thirty-fifth President of the United States.

Vermont—and New Englanders the principal subject matter of his poems. He was perhaps the most widely read and the best loved of all poets of his time.

The aged Frost could not see to read the poem he had prepared for the inauguration. He spoke from memory one of his older ones:

> The land was ours before we were the land's . . .
> Such as we were we gave ourselves outright
> (The deed of gift was many deeds of war)
> To the land vaguely realizing westward,
> But still unstoried, artless, unenhanced,
> Such as she was, such as she *will* become.

John F. Kennedy's entrance into national politics coincided with the re-entry of New England into the mainstream of American life. One of Kennedy's favorite words was "vigor." The vigorous, constructive realism he showed in his tragically short administration seemed to give official sanction to the efforts progressive New Englanders had been making to slough off their obsolete traditions.

Railroads and automobiles, the telephone, the radio, and the summer-resident industry had ended the isolation of New England towns, even though their inhabitants tried to keep the old symbols —the green with its meetinghouse, school, town hall, and free library—meaningful. The sacred institution of government by town meeting, and administration by public-spirited amateurs, had become another empty symbol. Skilled civil servants—accountants, school supervisors, welfare administrators, sanitation and highway experts—had had to be imported, in spite of local resistance to control from "outside."

The myth that the small rural community held the holy image of New England's independence had to fade. Technology had made the cities important. New England cities strove to catch up with the times.

Many streets in many New England cities were still little more than seventeenth-century lanes. Automobiles and trucks clogged them. In 1897, Boston had built America's first subway to get its inflexible streetcars off the surface, but fifty years later this under-

ground system badly needed extension. In Providence and New   *Robert Frost*
Haven, negotiating a city block in peak traffic required half an
hour. People who could afford to move went to the suburbs, taking
their tax money with them and leaving the cities financially helpless to correct transportation systems, attract business, and improve
housing.

In the mid-1930's Boston and Cambridge were filthy, antiquated
in every branch of city administration, and pockmarked with

and, after the war, the electronic programs and implements that would keep America ahead in the space-and-missile race.

The far-sighted real-estate firm of Cabot, Cabot and Forbes induced firms engaged in those fields to move to the "industrial parks" they were creating along Route 128. There the rural atmosphere would be pleasant for the scientists to work in, and the locations would be convenient to the less specialized workers from the Boston suburbs. Furthermore, the scientists could keep in touch with the intellectual and experimentational resources of the universities, and with one another. Thousands of workers were spared the tedium and expense of commuting into and out of the crowded city. Industries which might have been forced out of Massachusetts remained to make Route 128 the electronics capital of the nation.

A typical industrial park on Route 128 consists of several acres. The grounds, once swamp or substandard farmland, are landscaped with lawns and trees and, near the plant building itself, flower beds. The plant building is set back about a quarter-mile from the noise of the highway. It is broad and low, fork-lift shifting of warehouse goods having made elevators unnecessary. It may be surrounded with a decorative water-filled moat. It has been designed by a master architect, and it seems a cage of glass whose bars are of metal or of colorful masonry. Behind the building is a parking space with room reserved for workers' cars—many workers travel in car pools—and guests'. Raw materials are brought to these laboratories and leave as finished goods by night so that the campus-like atmosphere is not disturbed during major working hours. No goods or equipment clutter the grounds. Birds sing around the plants, and squirrels scamper in the trees.

The industrial-park idea has spread across the country as the New England Way began to do 150 years before the word electronics had been coined.

Technology also provided the means for Boston to remake itself in the modern image. Most of Boston's forty-eight square miles is "made" land. Bays, coves, and ponds were filled in when the old three-peaked hill, the "Trimountain," was cut down in the early nineteenth century. While other American cities were building skyscrapers to take care of the increase in their working and resi-

dential population, Boston believed it impossible to erect them on such an unstable foundation. Science destroyed this myth. Boston has considerably eased its congestion by putting up high-rise dwelling and business structures based on concrete piles sunk deep through the fill to bedrock granite. These are surrounded with open space, giving them light and air. Bostonians now have room to breathe.

The Art and Architecture Building at Yale was designed by Paul Rudolph, chairman of the department of architecture.

The beautiful parts of Boston have been preserved. The grace and dignity of their eighteenth- and early nineteenth-century houses and public buildings have been enhanced by the demolition of the dilapidated areas which had grown up like weeds around them. New structures designed by Walter Gropius, Jose Luis Sert, Pietro Belluschi, and the several firms who designed the new city hall adjoin the houses and churches of Bulfinch and Asher Benjamin and Richardson. These new buildings are free from the monotonous standardization of, say, New York City's curtain-wall skyscrapers of glass and steel; each is a unique and distinctive work by a master of modern architecture. Boston has combined its ancient and modern loveliness to become one of America's most beautiful, efficient, and esthetically stimulating cities.

Smaller Cambridge, across the Charles River, has become cos-

*Life insurance building,
Hartford*

mopolitan because of the sizable number of residents from all parts of the globe, attracted by its institutions of higher learning—Harvard, Radcliffe, M.I.T.—and Tufts, only four miles away. Many of the graduates of these institutions who come from other regions now stay in Greater Boston and hang out their shingles as lawyers, doctors, engineers, and other professionals.

Cambridge's Federal Period houses along Brattle Street, Bulfinch's and Richardson's Harvard buildings, and M.I.T.'s neoclassic main building have been punctuated with later twentieth-century construction. Cambridge is a veritable museum of exciting contemporary architecture in which almost all the masters are represented.

Hartford is another New England city which has responded to the challenge of the space age and yet kept its earlier monuments. Hartford's green glass Phoenix Mutual Life Insurance Company building is the first elliptical office building in the world. Hartford demolished much of its antiquated, ugly business section and replaced it with Constitution Plaza, a trim and handsome complex of shops, hotels, and office buildings—all surrounded by green parks and light and clean air.

New Haven has begun to remodel its grimy congested areas with gleaming modern buildings. The Yale campus has at last varied its traditional artificial Gothic with provocative new architectural creations.

There is, of course, much more to be done to completely revive New England from the lethargy of the pre-World War II years which made it the nation's odd old auntie. The renewal of its cities, accomplished by citizens still as community-minded as the founding Puritans, and by energetic civic executives like Boston's Mayor John F. Collins, is a revolution that has been effected by the same orderly means as the one that led to Lexington. A spotlight may now illuminate the chaste white meetinghouse on a New England town's Green to remind its saints—and strangers—of the old tradition. But a new integrity, free from the tyranny of myths, shines with its own warmer, farther-reaching light.

*Academic procession,
Brown University*

Reading About New England

One can visit New England in one's imagination through the many stories, biographies, and histories that have been written about it and its people.

The Pilgrims are best interpreted in Stephen Vincent Benet's fine narrative poem, *Western Star,* which follows closely William Bradford's record of the founding and the early days of the Plymouth colony.

Nathaniel Hawthorne's *Grandfather's Chair* gives a good picture of Puritan New England. Somewhat more complex, but an even better picture, is his *The Scarlet Letter.*

The colonial wars and the Revolution are thrillingly re-created in Kenneth Roberts's *Arundel, Northwest Passage,* and *Oliver Wiswell.* His *The Lively Lady* is about the War of 1812.

Extremely interesting is Esther Forbes's *Paul Revere and the World He Lived In.* Her novel about the Revolution, *Johnny Tremain,* is entertaining and accurate in detail.

Herman Melville's chronicle of whaling, *Moby Dick,* is one of the world's greatest novels. Richard Henry Dana's *Two Years Before the Mast* is a true story of a young man's life on one of the merchant ships of New England.

Rural New England after the Civil War is clearly revealed in Kate Douglas Wiggin's charming *Rebecca of Sunnybrook Farm,* and, more tragically, in Edith Wharton's *Ethan Frome.* William Dean Howells' *The Rise of Silas Lapham* is an excellent representation of life in Boston in the nineteenth century and of the New England character. For a somewhat later period, read Thornton Wilder's play about New England village life, *Our Town.*

The Brahmin is both satirically and sympathetically presented in John P. Marquand's novel, *The Late George Apley,* and in Cleveland Amory's *The Proper Bostonians.*

The works of Samuel Eliot Morison, one of America's finest historians, are extremely readable. Especially recommended are his *Builders of the Bay Colony, The Maritime History of Massachusetts,* and *Three Centuries of Harvard.* Catherine Drinker Bowen's life of Oliver Wendell Holmes, *Yankee from Olympus,* is a masterpiece of simple, penetrating biography. *Yankee Kingdom,* by Ralph Nading Hill, and *Massachusetts: There She Stands—Behold Her,* by Henry F. Howe, are good regional histories of Vermont and New Hampshire and of Massachusetts respectively.

Embroidered rug, Vermont

Some Important Dates

1497   John Cabot discovers Cape Breton Island and the New England coast.

1606   King James I grants a charter to the Plymouth Company of England for a colony in what is now New England.

1607   George Popham establishes a short-lived settlement in Maine at the mouth of the Kennebec River.

1614   Captain John Smith explores and maps the New England coast. He is the first to call the region by its present name. Publishes "A Description of New England," 1616.

1620   Pilgrims land at Provincetown (November 11). Mayflower Compact. Proceed to Plymouth (December 20).

1625   Miles Standish puts an end to Thomas Morton's Merrymount.

1628   John Endecott establishes a colony at Salem.

1630   Puritans settle in Boston (September 7).

1635   Puritans banish Roger Williams. He founds colony of Providence, 1636.

1636   Harvard College founded. Thomas Hooker founds Hartford.

1637   Anne Hutchinson banished from Boston. Pequot War in Connecticut.

1638   John Davenport and Theophilus Eaton found New Haven Colony. Portsmouth, Rhode Island, founded.

1639   "Fundamental Orders" of Connecticut. Newport founded.

1640   First book printed in North America, Richard Mather's *Bay Psalm Book.*

1643   Articles of Confederation signed by four New England colonies—Massachusetts Bay, Plymouth, Connecticut, and New Haven.

1644   Roger Williams obtains charter for Rhode Island.

1664   New Haven colony absorbed into Connecticut.

1675-76   King Philip's War.

1684   Massachusetts Bay Colony's charter voided. Sir Edmund Andros the Royal Governor of the colony, 1686.

1689-97   King William's War.

1690   Sir William Phips captures Port Royal, Nova Scotia.

1691   Massachusetts Bay Colony granted a new charter. Accepted, 1692.

1692   Plymouth joined with Massachusetts.

1693   Salem witchcraft trials and executions.

1701   Yale College founded.

1702-13   Queen Anne's War.

1704   Deerfield massacre.

1715   Massachusetts' first bank begins operations.

1744-48   King George's War. General period of the "Great Awakening."

1745   Capture of Louisbourg, Cape Breton Island.

1754-63   French and Indian War (in Europe, Seven Years' War, 1756-63).

1764   Rhode Island College (Brown University) founded.

1765   Sons of Liberty formed to oppose Stamp Act.

Tin weathervane

1768 British troops reinforce garrison in Boston.

1770 Dartmouth College founded. Boston Massacre.

1772 First Committee of Correspondence organized in Boston by Samuel Adams.

1773 Boston Tea Party.

1775 Battles of Lexington and Concord (April 19). Capture of Ticonderoga (May 10). Battle of Bunker Hill (June 17). George Washington takes command of Continental Army, Cambridge (July 3).

1776 British evacuate Boston (March 17). Declaration of Independence (July 4).

1777 Battle of Bennington.

1783 Treaty of Paris ends Revolutionary War (September 3).

1787 Shays' Rebellion quashed at Petersham, Massachusetts.

1790 The *Columbia* returns to Boston. Era of China trade begins.

1791 Vermont, an independent republic since 1777, enters the Union as the fourteenth state.

1794 Eli Whitney patents cotton gin. Later builds firearms factory near New Haven, to use new system of interchangeable parts.

1797 Inauguration of John Adams of Massachusetts as second U. S. President.

1803 War with Tripoli.

1807 Embargo Act recommended by President Jefferson and passed by Congress. Repealed, 1809.

1812-14 War of 1812.

1814 Hartford Convention.

1820-21 Maine enters the Union as a free state and Missouri as a slave state, as part of the Missouri Compromise.

1825 Inauguration of John Quincy Adams of Massachusetts as sixth U.S. President.

1846 Dr. William Morton performs first operation under anesthetic, at Massachusetts General Hospital.

1850 Fugitive Slave Law passed by Congress in reaction to the Underground Railroad.

1852 Death of Daniel Webster. Book publication of *Uncle Tom's Cabin* by Harriet Beecher Stowe.

1853 Inauguration of Franklin Pierce of New Hampshire as fourteenth U.S. President.

1854 William Lloyd Garrison publicly burns the U.S. Constitution.

1861-65 Civil War.

1865 Founding of M.I.T.

1875 Publication of Mary Baker Eddy's *Science and Health with Key to the Scriptures,* Christian Science textbook.

1876 Alexander Graham Bell patents the telephone.

1880-90 Decline of older New England industries begins.

1881 Inauguration of Chester A. Arthur, born in Vermont, as twenty-first U.S. President.

1902 Oliver Wendell Holmes of Harvard Law School appointed to U.S. Supreme Court.

1916 Louis D. Brandeis of Harvard Law School appointed to U.S. Supreme Court.

1917-18 U.S. participation in World War I.

1919 Boston police strike.

1921 Sacco-Vanzetti trial. Sacco and Vanzetti executed, 1927.

1923 Inauguration of Vermont-born Calvin Coolidge of Massachusetts as thirtieth U.S. President.

1926 Robert H. Goddard launches first liquid-fuel rocket near Worcester.

1929 Great Depression begins.

1938 Great hurricane (September).

1941-45 U.S. participation in World War II.

1961 Inauguration of John F. Kennedy of Massachusetts as thirty-fifth U.S. President.

NOTE: Biographical dates of important New Englanders appear following their names in the index.

Index

176

ABOUT THE AUTHOR—Monroe Stearns is an eleventh-generation descendant of Richard Mather, who settled in New England in 1635. Mr. Stearns went to school in Worcester and Boston, as well as to Harvard College. Later he taught in boys' schools in Connecticut (Simsbury and Salisbury) and Massachusetts (Sheffield) and lectured on American literature in Rhode Island (Brown University). He has summered in three New England states—New Hampshire (White Mountains), Massachusetts (Martha's Vineyard and Boston's North Shore), and Maine (Moosehead Lake and Mount Desert Island).

Mr. Stearns has been managing editor of Bobbs-Merrill, an editor at Prentice-Hall, and Director of Public Information for UNICEF. His dozen books include *Ring-a-Ling, The Key to Rome,* and *Mark Twain.*